Color Scanning Handbook
Your Guide to Hewlett-Packard ScanJet Color Scanners

Hewlett-Packard Professional Books

Atchison	Object-Oriented Test & Measurement Software Development in C++
Blinn	Portable Shell Programming: An Extensive Collection of Bourne Shell Examples
Blommers	Practical Planning for Network Growth
Caruso	Power Programming in HP OpenView: Developing CMIS Applications
Cook	Building Enterprise Information Architectures
Costa	Planning and Designing High Speed Networks Using 100VG-AnyLAN, Second Edition
Crane	A Simplified Approach to Image Processing: Classical and Modern Techniques
Day	Color Scanning Handbook: Your Guide to Hewlett-Packard ScanJet Color Scanners
Fernandez	Configuring the Common Desktop Environment
Fristrup	USENET: Netnews for Everyone
Fristrup	The Essential Web Surfer Survival Guide
Grady	Practical Software Metrics for Project Management and Process Improvement
Grosvenor, Ichiro, O'Brien	Mainframe Downsizing to Upsize Your Business: IT-Preneuring
Gunn	A Guide to NetWare® for UNIX®
Helsel	Graphical Programming: A Tutorial for HP VEE
Helsel	Visual Programming with HP VEE, Second Edition
Holman, Lund	Instant JavaScript
Kane	PA-RISC 2.0 Architecture
Knouse	Practical DCE Programming
Lee	The ISDN Consultant: A Stress-Free Guide to High-Speed Communications
Lewis	The Art & Science of Smalltalk
Lund	Integrating UNIX® and PC Network Operating Systems
Madell	Disk and File Management Tasks on HP-UX
Mahoney	High-Mix Low-Volume Manufacturing
Malan, Letsinger, Coleman	Object-Oriented Development at Work: Fusion in the Real World
McFarland	X Windows on the World: Developing Internationalized Software with X, Motif®, and CDE
McMinds/Whitty	Writing Your Own OSF/Motif Widgets
Norton, DiPasquale	Thread Time: The Multithreaded Programming Guide
Orzessek, Sommer	Digital Video: An Introduction to Digital Video Services in Broadband Networks
Phaal	LAN Traffic Management
Pipkin	Halting the Hacker: A Practical Guide to Computer Security
Poniatowski	The HP-UX System Administrator's "How To" Book
Poniatowski	HP-UX 10.x System Administration "How To" Book
Poniatowski	Learning the HP-UX Operating System
Poniatowski	The Windows NT and HP-UX System Administrator's How-To Book
Ryan	Distributed Object Technology: Concepts and Applications
Thomas	Cable Television Proof-of-Performance: A Practical Guide to Cable TV Compliance Measurements Using a Spectrum Analyzer
Weygant	Clusters for High Availability: A Primer of HP-UX Solutions
Witte	Electronic Test Instruments
Yawn, Stachnick, Sellars	The Legacy Continues: Using the HP 3000 with HP-UX and Windows NT

Color Scanning Handbook

Your Guide to Hewlett-Packard ScanJet Color Scanners

Jerry B. Day

Hewlett-Packard Company

To join a Prentice Hall PTR Internet mailing list, point to
http://www.prenhall.com/register

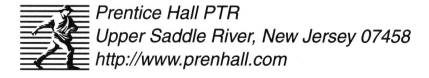

Prentice Hall PTR
Upper Saddle River, New Jersey 07458
http://www.prenhall.com

Library of Congress Cataloging in Publication Data

Day, Jerry B.
    Color scanning handbook : your guide to Hewlett-Packard ScanJet color / Jerry B.
  Day : Hewlett-Packard Company.
        p.   cm
    Includes bibliographical references and index.
    ISBN 0-13-375211-0 (alk. paper)
    1. HP ScanJet scanners. 2. Scanning systems. 3. Color separation.
    I. Hewlett-Packard Company. II. Title.
TK7882.S3D36   1997
006.6'2--dc21   97-19529
                                           CIP

Editorial/Production Supervision: *Kathleen M. Caren*
Cover Design Director: *Jerry Votta*
Manufacturing Manager: *Alexis Heydt*
Marketing Manager: *Miles Williams*
Acquisitions Editor: *Karen Gettman*
Editorial Assistant: *Barbara Alfieri*
Manager, Hewlett-Packard Press: *Patricia Pekary*

Published by Prentice Hall PTR
Prentice-Hall, Inc.
A Simon & Schuster Company
Upper Saddle River, New Jersey 07458

Prentice Hall books are widely used by corporations and government agencies for training, marketing, and resale. The publisher offers discounts on this book when ordered in bulk quantities.
For more information, contact Corporate Sales Department, Phone: 800-382-3419;
FAX: 201-236-7141; email: corpsales@prenhall.com
Prentice Hall PTR, One Lake Street, Upper Saddle River, NJ 07458.

Printed in the United States of America
10 9 8 7 6 5 4 3 2

ISBN 0-13-357211-0

Prentice-Hall International (UK) Limited, *London*
Prentice-Hall of Australia Pty. Limited, *Sydney*
Prentice-Hall Canada Inc., *Toronto*
Prentice-Hall Hispanoamericana, S.A., *Mexico*
Prentice-Hall of India Private Limited, *New Delhi*
Prentice-Hall of Japan, Inc., *Tokyo*
Simon & Schuster Asia Pte. Ltd., *Singapore*
Editora Prentice-Hall do Brasil, Ltda., *Rio de Janeiro*

Contents

About the Author

*J*erry Day has been a senior technical writer and publications project manager at Hewlett-Packard for nine years. He was technical publications project manager for the HP ScanJet 3c and 4c and is currently managing publications for a new scanner to be introduced in the near future. His previous works include *Super Scanning Techniques* by HP Press and Random House. Prior to his work on scanners, Jerry produced technical publications on a variety of subjects including UNIX networking software, computer graphics software, photographic processing equipment, and video editing systems.

In a previous life, Jerry was a U.S. Air Force professional photographer for more than twenty years. He was an instructor in the Air Force photography school for more than six years. In the late 1970's, he was the audiovisual manager and chief of photography for the U.S. Air Force in Europe.

Jerry has spoken on desktop publishing, scanning, the tracing process, Adobe PostScript, Adobe Acrobat, and multimedia project management to such groups as the Hewlett-Packard technical publication managers conference, the International CorelDRAW User Conference, the Ventura Publisher User's Conference, the Corel Splash 95 conference in London, and the Society for Technical Communication's national conference in Atlanta and STC regional conferences in Denver and Portland, Oregon.

Jerry and his wife Anne live in Louisville, Colorado (north of Denver and near Boulder). Although he no longer works as a professional photographer, he still heads for the mountains with his Nikons whenever he can to photograph the beautiful scenery and Colorado's fascinating narrow gauge steam trains.

Dedication

*T*his book is dedicated to Anne, my wife of 33 years. Everything that I am and still hope to be, I owe to God and to her. Thanks for the words of encouragement when the technical words wouldn't come (I think they call it writer's block).

This book is also dedicated to my son Tim and his wife Debbie, who recently became parents making me a grand dad. Thanks Tim for all those wonderful times we had when you were so young, chasing those old trains, climbing around the mountains looking for just the right picture.

Acknowledgments

I would like to thank all of the many individuals who contributed to this book in so many ways. My special gratitude to Kevin Bier and David Huss who took time from their busy schedules to make sure everything was technically correct (any errors or mistakes are mine and not theirs). Thanks to the thousands of wonderful folks who use HP ScanJet scanners to produce so many exciting and interesting projects—they provided the inspiration to produce this book. My appreciation to all of the people and companies who so freely and willingly provided the information and products necessary to complete this book. Thanks to David Huss and Gary Bouton for copies of their books on *Corel PHOTO-PAINT* and *Adobe Photoshop*. Thanks also to the folks at Adobe Systems and Alien Skin software for letting me test their excellent products. For the drawings of the HP CDR drive, thanks to Cindy Butler and Mike Bemis of Hewlett-Packard's Colorado Memory Systems division. Special thanks to Karen Gettman and the staff at Prentice Hall who were involved in producing *The Color Scanning Handbook*. And to Paul Cackowski, thanks for the drawings; but especially, thanks for being a good friend.

Introduction

A s the price of color desktop printers decreases and the quality of desktop color printing increases, more personal, business, and technical publications are being printed in color. People like color! It is real and natural and is expected by readers today. *The Color Scanning Handbook* provides information on scanning drawings and photographs in both color and in black-and-white. This book is designed to be a supplement to the user guides that accompany each Hewlett-Packard ScanJet scanner. This book provides information applicable to HP ScanJet scanners that support the HP DeskScan II software. The material is applicable to both Apple Macintosh computers as well as computers using Microsoft Windows 3.1 or 95.

The Color Scanning Handbook is intended to provide instructions, information, and tips to help you to be productive and creative with your HP ScanJet scanner. I hope that this book also provides information that will show you how to have fun with it!

In this Book

*T*his book shows you how to get more from your HP ScanJet scanner and how to use it in ways you may not have thought of.

Chapter 1 "How Color Works" describes how color works in the real world and in color photography and imaging.

Chapter 2 "How Color Scanning Works" describes what a color scanner is and how one works.

Chapter 3 "How to Select an Image Type" explains how to select an image type for your scanned images.

Chapter 4 "How to Select a File Format" describes the various file format types and explains how to select one of the formats for your images.

Chapter 5 "How to Get the Best Color Scan" explains how to use the DeskScan II tools and controls to produce the best scanned image.

Chapter 6 "How to Use Scanned Images with Software Applications" provides information on how to use your scanned images with software applications such as word processors, image editors, etc.

Chapter 7 "How to Scan for the Computer Screen" describes the process of scanning color images for online documentation, for multimedia presentations, for computer networks, etc.

Chapter 8 "How to Trace a Scanned Image" describes the process of converting bitmapped images to a vector format by using tracing software.

Chapter 9 "How To...Scanning Tips & Techniques" provides a selection of tips and tricks to help you to be more productive and have fun with your scanner.

Chapter 10 "How to Print Scanned Images" explains how to print your scanned images on desktop printers and how to use your desktop printer as a proofing device.

Chapter 11 "How to Print Scanned Images on a Printing Press" explains how to print on high-resolution devices and how to get your images printed on commercial printing presses.

Chapter 12 "References" lists books, magazines, plug-in filters, and clip art sources that will help you get more from your scanner.

Conventions Used in this Book

Special Text or Fonts

In this book, I used the following special text or type to help identify what actions you are required to take to make your HP ScanJet scanner work:

- Text that you enter or menus you click on are indicated with **bold text**.
  Example: Click on **OK**.

- Terms that are described for the first time are indicated by *italics*. Also, all tips, cautions, and references to other sections are indicated with italics.
  Example: Scan the image using *TWAIN*.

- Text that is displayed on the computer screen is indicated with the `Courier` typeface.
  Example: The DOS file extension for TIFF is `.TIF`.

Icon Aids

This book uses cartoon-like icons in the margin to provide visual indicators of tips, cautions, or additional information.

This is a good thing to do! A tip is my recommendation for a procedure or method of using your HP ScanJet scanner to get the best results.

There is more to it! This icon indicates that additional information that is not part of the current text is available either elsewhere in this book or in the resources listed in Chapter 12.

Don't do this. These will be my recommendations for things that you should avoid, or in some cases, will be a recommendation of an alternative way of doing something.

Don't forget this! These are things that I think you should make a special effort to remember. Of course I would like for you to remember the entire book, but I know that is not realistic…my wife doesn't even remember it all!

Get Clicking with Your Mouse

Because this book is for both Macintosh and Windows users, I generally provide instructions using the mouse rather than the keyboard because of the differences between the two types of keyboards. I will usually tell you to click the mouse, or to double-click the mouse. Clicking the mouse on a menu item or an object selects that item or object. Double-clicking with the mouse is usually the same as clicking the mouse on a dialog and then clicking on OK (double-clicking saves a mouse click). If you are just beginning with computers or haven't used the mouse a lot, refer to the user documentation for your computer for instructions on how to use your particular type of mouse.

Keep Your DeskScan II Software Up-to-Date

*H*ewlett-Packard regularly updates the DeskScan II software that accompanied your HP ScanJet scanner. If you purchased your HP ScanJet scanner several years ago, there have been a number of changes to the DeskScan II software.

This book illustrates and describes the current version of the software. You should always have and use the latest version. The latest version will contain any new features that have been added as well as fixes to any problems in the previous version (I don't like to use the word "bug"). You can obtain the latest version directly from HP for a nominal fee. You can also download the latest version electronically at no charge from HP's Web site on the Internet or from the HP forums on America Online and CompuServe.

For information on obtaining updated software or how to access the HP electronic services, consult the Installation Guide that accompanied your HP ScanJet scanner.

How to Determine What Version of DeskScan II You Are Using:

So, how do you know what version of DeskScan II you have?

1. Click on **Help** in the DeskScan II menu.

2. Click on **About DeskScan II...**

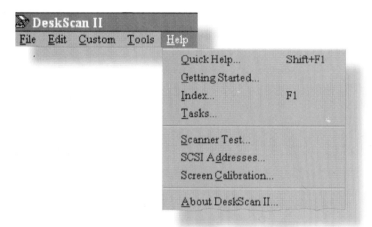

3. The following screen will be displayed. The version number is shown in the lower right-hand side of the screen. At the time this book was produced, the current version was 2.4.

Chapter 1

How
Color Works

Introduction

*T*o get the most from your HP ScanJet color scanner and to understand how color scanning and color printing work, you should have a basic understanding of how we see color and how color is created photographically and electronically. Knowing how color works in the natural world and how this natural world is recreated with film and paper will help you appreciate both the excitement of color on the desktop as well as some of the limitations.

Light and Color

*W*ithout light, nothing is visible to the human eye or to photographic film and there is no color (for this discussion, I have omitted infrared, ultraviolet, and other forms of light that are not visible to the human eye). Light is radiant energy that moves in waves. Each color of light has a different wavelength (measured from the top of one wave to the top of the next wave).

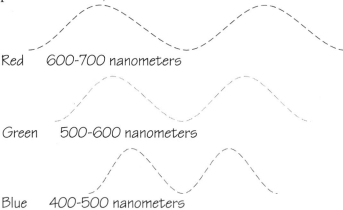

Red   600-700 nanometers

Green   500-600 nanometers

Blue   400-500 nanometers

Light moves in waves. White light is made up of equal parts of red, green, and blue light. Each color has a different wavelength. Wavelengths longer than 700 nanometers (infrared) or shorter than 400 nanometers (ultraviolet) are invisible to the human eye.

Don't worry, this is not physics 101, and you don't have to remember all of these numbers! The important thing to remember is that light is energy and the color that we see and that is recorded physically, chemically, and digitally is light. To understand how color works, you must first understand a few simple basics of how light works.

As light radiates from its origin to strike an object, it is either reflected by the object, absorbed by the object, or transmitted (through transparent or semi-transparent objects).

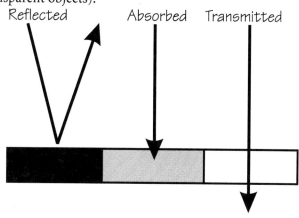

When visible light strikes an object, it is reflected, absorbed, or transmitted. If the object reflects equal proportions of red, green, and blue light, the object will appear white. If the object absorbs all of the light, it will appear black.

Depending on the physical characteristics of an object, all of the light striking the object may be reflected, absorbed, or transmitted; or, some of the light may be reflected, some absorbed, and some transmitted. When white light strikes a lemon, the blue light is absorbed and the red and green light are reflected. We see the lemon as yellow because the red and green light reflected from it combine to create yellow. The windshield of an

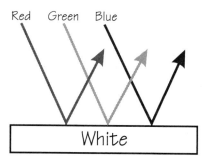
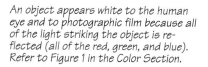

An object appears white to the human eye and to photographic film because all of the light striking the object is reflected (all of the red, green, and blue). Refer to Figure 1 in the Color Section.

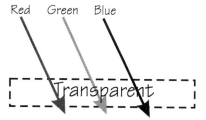

The windshield of a car is transparent to the human eye because all of the light that strikes it is transmitted through it (tinted windshields don't count). Refer to Figure 2 in the Color Section.

automobile appears clear because the glass transmits all of the red, green, and blue light striking it.

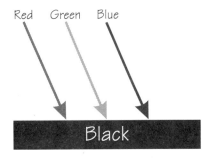

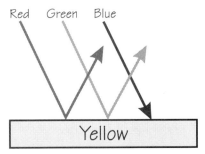

This object appears black to the eye and to film because all of the light striking the object is absorbed. To see this illustration in color, refer to Figure 3 in the Color Section.

This object appears yellow to the eye and to film because the blue component of white light is absorbed while the red and green, which combine to produce yellow, are reflected. Refer to Figure 4 in the Color Section.

Color Models

*T*wo models are used to predominately produce (and explain) color photography, color scanning, and color printing:

- *Additive color* (also known as RGB)
  Used by computer display monitors and color scanners.
- *Subtractive color* (also known as CMYK)
  Used in photographic color film and prints, and also used in four-color publishing and printing.

Additive Color (RGB)

This model is called the additive process because colors are produced by adding (or combining) one or more colors to produce additional colors. In the additive model, color is created by adding different amounts of red, green, and blue light.

Pure white light is composed of equal proportions of red, green, and blue light. Red, green, and blue (also called RGB by photographers and graphic designers) are called *additive primary* colors because when they are combined (or added) they produce all other colors. For example, combine equal amounts of red and green light and the color yellow is produced. The reason a lemon is yellow is because when it is struck by white light, the blue portion of the white light is absorbed and the red and green are reflected. The absence of all light produces black. So, a black object absorbs all (or most) of the white light. The color of an object is determined by which colors are reflected, absorbed, or transmitted when light strikes the object.

For the moment, forget what you learned about mixing colors with paint. Paint pigments do not mix the way light does. The primary and secondary colors of color painting are not the same primary and secondary colors we will be discussing in color photography, color scanning, and color printing.

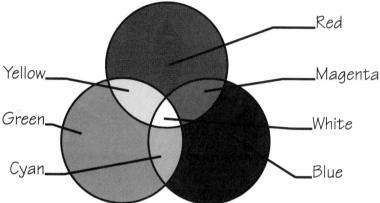

The additive color model. When two of the primary colors are combined, they produce one of the secondary colors. For example, red and green combined produce yellow. When all three additive primary colors are combined, they produce white. To see this image in color, refer to Figure 5 in the Color Section.

The first color photographic images were produced using the additive process in 1861 by James Clerk Maxwell. This was the first known demonstration of color photography. Maxwell made three black-and-white negatives of the same scene through photographic filters. Each filter transmitted one of the additive primary colors (red, green, and blue). Each negative represented one part of the scene that was red, green, or blue. The red negative, for example, only contained parts of the scene that were red. Next, Maxwell made a positive copy of each negative on photographic film. Then, using three theater spotlights, he projected each negative onto a screen through a filter (for example, the red negative was projected through a red filter). When the three projected images were precisely aligned on the screen, a full-color image resulted.

Subtractive Color (CMYK)

The subtractive color model is so named because color is subtracted from white light to produce other colors. The subtractive color model uses the secondary colors (cyan, magenta, and yellow). You will see this model referred to as the CMYK model. The K is added because a combination of 100% cyan, magenta, and yellow ink cannot produce a pure black when producing printed matter with a color printing press. A mixture of 100% cyan, magenta, and yellow ink will produce a muddy-looking brown. Black ink is added to compensate for this inability, hence the CMYK. You might ask why isn't B used for black? B is already used for blue, so K is used for black (they used the last letter instead of the first in this case).

The subtractive color model is the basis for almost all conventional color photography and commercial color printing. The reason it is used instead of the additive model is due to limitations of the color dyes used in color photography and inks used in four-color commercial printing. Cyan, magenta, and yellow dyes and inks transmit light better and are more chemically stable than red, green, and blue dyes and inks.

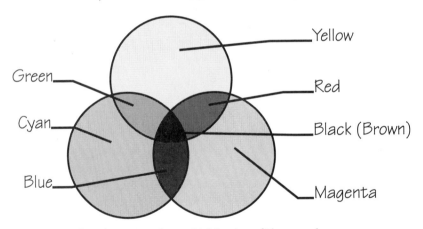

The subtractive color model. When two of the secondary colors are combined, they produce one of the primary colors. For example, yellow and cyan combined produce green. When all three subtractive secondary colors are combined, they produce black. Refer to Figure 6 in the Color Section.

To understand how only three colors of dye or ink can be used to produce the full range of colors seen in nature, first remember this rule: *color dye or ink will transmit its own color and absorb all other colors.* The illustration shows how this works. The cyan transmits green and blue because green and blue combined produce cyan. The cyan absorbs red. The magenta transmits red and blue because magenta is made up of red and blue.

Magenta absorbs green. In photographic film and paper, and in the commercial printing process, three layers of cyan, magenta, and yellow are placed on top of each other (commercial printing adds black ink). These three layers filter the white light striking the film, photographic paper, or printed page to create the appropriate color for each part of the image.

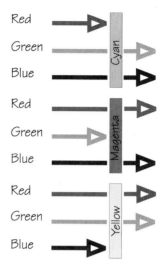

How Color Photography Works

*C*olor photography utilizes the subtractive color model to produce color negatives, color prints, and color transparencies (commonly known as slides...although they are also produced in sizes other than 35mm, such as 4 inch by 5 inch).

All color photography begins with film or paper bases coated with light-sensitive photographic silver. Photographic film and papers have three layers of this light-sensitive silver. Each layer is made sensitive to one of the additive primary colors.

Red   Green   Blue   Cyan   Magenta   Yellow   White   Black

Blue-sensitive silver

Green-sensitive silver

Red-sensitive silver

Film Base

When red light strikes this photographic film or paper, the red is recorded only in the red-sensitive layer. Blue is recorded in the blue-sensitive layer and so on. When one of the subtractive colors (cyan, magenta, or yellow)

strikes the photographic material, it is recorded in two of the light-sensitive layers. Remember, the subtractive colors are made up of two of the additive colors. Cyan is recorded in the blue- and green-sensitive layers because cyan is made from blue and green. White light is recorded in all three layers because red, green, and blue combine to produce white. Black is not recorded in any layer, because black is the absence of light. Colors such as brown, orange, pink, etc. are mixtures of the additive and subtractive colors.

When exposed photographic material is chemically processed, the light-sensitive silver layers are converted to dye layers. The blue-sensitive silver layer is converted to yellow dye, the green layer is converted to magenta dye, and the red layer is converted to cyan dye. In photographic negatives and transparencies the yellow layer is on top, magenta in the middle, and cyan on the bottom. In photographic paper prints, the layers are reversed. This is because light is transmitted by negatives and transparencies and light is reflected by photographic prints. The light actually passes through the dye layers in photographic prints twice.

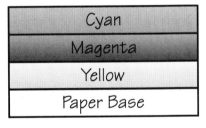

The dye layers in photographic negatives and positive transparencies. Refer to Figure 8 in the Color Section.

The dye layers in photographic paper prints. Refer to Figure 9 in the Color Section.

Now let's see how all of this works by photographing a simple object and seeing how it is recorded in a photographic negative and in a normal photographic print like the ones from the drug store, one-hour lab, or professional photo lab. For the sake of illustration, we will photograph a yellow ball.

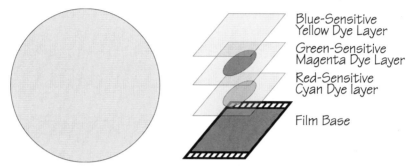

Blue-Sensitive
Yellow Dye Layer

Green-Sensitive
Magenta Dye Layer

Red-Sensitive
Cyan Dye layer

Film Base

Remember, yellow is composed of equal parts of red and green. When we photograph a yellow object, it is recorded in the red and green layers of the color film (in this case, color negative film). So, the yellow ball is recorded in the green- and red-sensitive layers of the film and is composed of magenta and cyan dye.

When color negative film is processed, it has an orange cast to it. I am sure you have tried to look at color negative film and have had difficulty determining colors due to to all the orange. This cast is caused by special dyes that are added to the film base to compensate for deficiencies in the normal dyes used in photographic film.

All that should be left in color film are the three dye layers (cyan, magenta, and yellow). However, even the best available dyes absorb some of the light which they should transmit. For example, a perfect cyan dye would absorb only red light and would transmit green and blue light. All known cyan dyes, however, absorb fairly large portions of green and blue light. Similarly, a perfect magenta dye would absorb only green light, transmitting blue and red light.

Color negatives are hard to look at, and you can't send a copy to your grandmother, so you have color prints made. Color prints consist of the same three dye layers coated on a sheet of paper. The dye layers are reversed, the red-sensitive layer is on top, the green-sensitive layer is still in the middle, and the blue-sensitive is on the bottom. Color prints are produced by shining white light through the color negative onto photographic paper (inside of a darkroom or photographic printing machine).

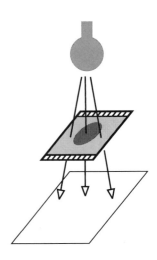

Red-Sensitive
Cyan Dye layer

Green-Sensitive
Magenta Dye Layer

Blue-Sensitive
Yellow Dye Layer

Paper Base

The yellow ball is blue on the photographic negative (blue is the opposite of yellow) and is composed of magenta and cyan dye. When the negative is exposed to white light, the magenta absorbs green, the cyan absorbs red, leaving blue light to strike the photographic paper. The blue light is recorded in the blue-sensitive layer which produces yellow dye when the paper is processed. When you view the color print, the yellow dye reflects yellow light to your eyes and you see the yellow ball.

Hue, Saturation, and Value

*O*ther color terms that you will need to understand include *hue*, *saturation*, and *value* (or brightness). You need to understand these terms to know how color works in the real word and in the world of photography and digital imaging. Let me begin with a definition of each term:

- **Hue**
  Hue (not Hugh the Borg on StarTrek) describes individual colors; for example, red objects are said to have a red hue.

- **Saturation**
  Saturation describes how intense or weak a color is...how red is the red?

- **Value** (or brightness)
  This describes the amount of light reflected from an object or
  how dark or light a scanned image is.

It is also important to understand these terms as the HP DeskScan II
software that accompanies your HP ScanJet scanner includes controls for
each of these.

Color Gamut

*T*o understand how color works in scanning and photography, it is
important to realize that in reproducing the real world with photographic film or with numbers, as in digital imaging, there are limitations.
There are a lot more colors out there in the real world than photographic
films or digital imaging can capture.

The technical term for this range of colors is *gamut*. There are several
gamuts. Photographic film has a gamut, meaning the range of colors that
can be captured by color photographic film. The widest gamut is actually
the human eye. We can see more colors than can be represented by
photographic film, computer monitors, or printed on paper. Following is
a list of the number of colors that can be seen or reproduced:

- The human eye can see billions of colors.

- A computer monitor can display sixteen million colors.

- Color photographic film can capture ten to fifteen thousand
  colors.

- A high-quality, four-color printing press can reproduce from five
  to six thousand colors.

The following illustration shows how each of these is related. The entire shaded area represents the area of light visible to the human eye. The areas inside represent how much of the visible light can be displayed or reproduced by each of the media.

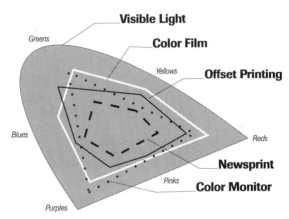

I hope this introductory chapter has helped you to understand how color works in the real world, in photography, and in digital imaging with your HP ScanJet scanner. Now that you have a basic understanding of how color works, you are ready to learn how your HP ScanJet scanner works in the next chapter.

Chapter 2

How Color
Scanning Works

Introduction

*T*his chapter will help you to understand what a scanner is and what one does. You don't really have to understand the inner workings of a scanner, just as you don't have to be a mechanic to drive a car. However, just as you would probably be a better driver if you knew the capabilities (and limitations) of your car, you will probably get better results if you have at least essential knowledge of what your HP ScanJet scanner is and what it can do.

What Is a Scanner?

A scanner is sometimes compared to the copy machine found in almost every office. Sometimes scanners are compared to cameras. A scanner uses technology that was first developed for office copy machines, but that is not a good comparison in that a scanner can store an image in a file.

A Scanner Is Like a Camera

A scanner is probably best compared to a photographic camera. Scanners and cameras both capture light that is reflected from an original subject. Cameras capture images with light-sensitive film and scanners do it with numbers (electronically).

How Do Cameras and Film Work?

Cameras use a lens and a shutter to focus the light and to control the amount of light that enters the camera. The camera stores the image in silver halide crystals coated on the surface of a sheet or roll of film. The film consists of an acetate base with millions of crystals of light-sensitive silver halide embedded in a layer of gelatin. Conventional photography is only possible because silver can be made to be light-sensitive. Color images are produced by converting the silver image to a series of dye layers.

When you take a picture with your camera, light is reflected from the subject through the camera lens when you snap the shutter. Normal subjects reflect different amounts of light. The dark areas of the scene reflect little or no light and the other areas reflect greater amounts of light. As light strikes the light-sensitive silver halide in the film, the electrical charge of each crystal is changed. When the film is developed, the crystals

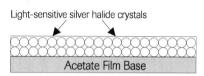

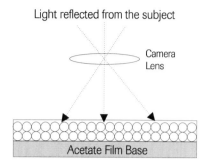

Photographic film (both color and B&W) consists of billions of silver halide crystals in a layer of gelatin that is coated on an acetate film base.

When the camera's shutter opens, light passes through the lens and strikes the light-sensitive silver halide in the film.

that were struck with light are changed to a black metallic silver and the ones that were not struck with light are washed from the film.

If you were to look at a piece of processed photographic film under a powerful microscope, you would see that there are varying amounts of silver deposited on the film base. Some areas of the film are thicker than others. Color films (slides and negatives) work in a similar manner except that they have three silver layers, each sensitive to a different color. During processing, the metallic silver halides are converted into one of three colors of dye.

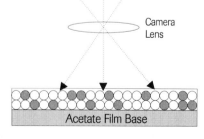

Subjects being photographed reflect varying amounts of light. Some parts of the film receive no light and others receive a lot of light.

After being processed, the silver halide crystals that were struck with light are made black. The ones that were not struck with light are removed chemically.

How Does a Scanner Work?

Scanners also record images by capturing reflected light through a lens. Your HP ScanJet scanner does not use film. The scanner has its own built-in light source (a special type of lamp). When you scan an image, the lamp shines light on the original (drawing, photograph, or document), which is placed on the scanner glass. The light is reflected from the original to a special computer chip called a *Charge-Couple Device* (CCD). The CCD detects the different amounts of light reflecting from different parts of the original. Dark areas reflect less light than light areas. Your HP ScanJet color scanner is equipped with CCDs for each of the three primary colors (red, green, and blue). They can detect different colors as well as levels of brightness of these three primaries. The CCDs in your scanner are essentially equivalent to the film in a camera.

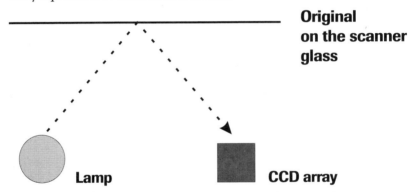

Original on the scanner glass

Lamp

CCD array

The electronic circuitry of the scanner converts the light to numbers. The scanner stores the image as a grid of squares using a series of numbers. Each square in the grid (called a pixel) is assigned a number based on its color and brightness. These numbers are called binary digits or *bits*. A single bit has two states: on or off. Off is indicated by a zero. A zero represents white. On is indicated by a one. A one represents black. To represent other colors or shades of gray, combinations of ones and zeroes are used. Computers can only work with these ones and zeroes and scanned images consist of a grid or map of numbers, hence the term *bitmap*. A bitmapped image then is a mathematical map of the pixels.

To understand how scanners create images represented by numbers and the concept of a bitmap, let's start with the simplest type of bitmap: the 1-bit black-and-white image. Look at how a scanner captures the image of a black-and-white drawing. On the left, I scanned a piece of clip art. It was saved as a 1-bit image, meaning that it only has ones and zeros in the image. On the right, I enlarged the image so that you can see the actual pixels. There are only black and white pixels in this image. The areas that were black in the original artwork were recorded as ones and the areas that were white were recorded as zeros.

If we were photographing the clip art with film, the areas that were white would be thick on the photograph negative and the areas that were black would be thin or blank. Film records images with thickness of silver on a piece of photographic film. Scanners record the different areas of images with different numbers rather than thickness of silver.

To record images that are more than just black and white, scanners use a concept called pixel depth. The scanner needs more than just two bits to record different levels of gray or color. To record levels of gray, scanners use 1, 4, 8, 16, and 24 bits to represent each pixel. This numbering system is deceiving though. A 4-bit scanned image records more than four shades of gray or color. Pixel depth is exponential. A 4-bit image does not record four times more than a 1-bit image, it records 16 times more. The following list shows how many shades of gray or color are recorded by each bit level:

- A 1-bit level pixel records only black and white.
- A 4-bit level pixel records 16 colors or shades of gray (4x4=16).
- An 8-bit level pixel records 256 colors or shades of gray (8x8=256).
- A 16-bit level pixel records 65,536 colors (16x16=65,536).

- A 24-bit level pixel records 16,777,216 colors (ScanJet just says "millions").

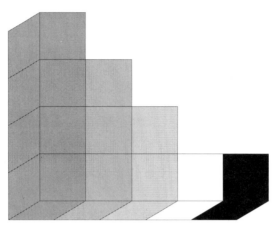

Illustration of pixel depth. Each square (or pixel) is represented by a number or bit. Black and white only require one number (a 0 or a 1). Shades of gray require more bits (or greater depth).

An important thing to keep in mind—pixel depth is a concept used to explain a fairly complex process. Pixel depth is a theoretical explanation used to describe how numbers are used to record levels of color and gray. A 256-level gray scale image has a greater depth (more bits) than a 16-level gray scale image. This concept is really all you need for a basic understanding of how your scanner works. I don't understand everything about how my automobile works, but I can drive it to work most of the time (flat tires don't count). Now that you know everything (???) about scanning, let's learn how it all started.

A Bit of Hewlett-Packard Scanner History

Hewlett-Packard introduced its first scanner, the HP ScanJet, in 1987. The HP ScanJet was 300 pixels-per-inch, black-and-white, with 16 levels of gray. This first model included HP Scanning Gallery software for Windows and HP Desk Scan for the Apple Macintosh.

In 1989, the HP ScanJet Plus replaced the original ScanJet. The HP ScanJet Plus was also a 300 ppi, black-and-white scanner, but it provided 256 levels of gray. The HP ScanJet

Plus also offered an *Automatic Document Feeder* (ADF) for use with Optical Character Recognition (OCR) software. The HP ScanJet and HP ScanJet Plus are no longer produced.

HP ScanJet IIp and 3p

HP offered a couple of other 300 ppi, black-and-white scanners: the HP ScanJet IIp and 3p, but they are no longer available. The IIp was introduced in 1991. It was replaced by the 3p in 1994. The 3p featured two new scanning software programs: HP PictureScan for scanning and HP PicturePlace for image editing. It also included Calera WordScan OCR software and HP Copier software. An optional ADF was offered.

HP ScanJet IIc

The HP ScanJet IIc, HP's first color scanner, was introduced in August of 1991. The HP ScanJet IIc was a 400 ppi, black-and-white and color desktop model that featured new image scanning software—HP DeskScan II for both Windows and Apple Macintosh. It also featured a new higher-capacity document feeder for OCR. Image editing software was included as well. Zedcor's DeskPaint was provided for Mac users. ZSoft's Publisher's Paintbrush and later ZSoft PhotoFinish were provided for Windows users. OCR software was provided for both the Macintosh and Windows versions.

HP ScanJet IIcx

The HP ScanJet IIcx was introduced in November 1993. The HP ScanJet IIcx was a replacement for the IIc. It featured increased speed and an optional adapter for scanning transparencies such as 35mm slides (Transparency Adapter). A new version of HP DeskScan II (version 2.0) offered several new features including ADF support, HP Accu-Page 2.0 for better OCR accuracy, and improvements to the TWAIN interface standard. New image editing software included Adobe Photoshop LE for Macintosh and Aldus PhotoStyler SE for Windows. OCR capability was provided with Macintosh and Windows versions of Calera WordScan software. HP Copier software allowed you to use your IIcx as a copy machine.

HP ScanJet 3c

In April of 1995, HP released the HP ScanJet 3c. This model featured 600 ppi resolution. Resolution could be increased to 2400 ppi using a special software enhancement called *interpolation*. It was 30-bit internal color capable of producing over one billion colors and 10-bit internal grayscale capable of producing 1024 levels of gray. As with the IIcx, ADF and Transparency Adapter options were offered. Corel PHOTO-PAINT image editor was provided for Windows users and Adobe Photoshop LE for Apple Macintosh users. Windows and Macintosh versions of Calera WordScan OCR software was also provided. HP ScanJet Copy software provided the capability for Macintosh and Windows users to use their scanner as a copy machine.

HP ScanJet 4c

The HP ScanJet 4c was introduced in November of 1995. It replaced the HP ScanJet 3c. The 4c included upgraded DeskScan II software with support for Microsoft Windows 95 and up-graded versions of Corel PHOTO-PAINT and HP Scan-Jet Copy. The Macintosh version included Adobe Photoshop LE. The 4C also came bundled with Visioneer PaperPort software that provided the capability to fax and email scanned images, Caere Omni-Page Limited Edition provided OCR support.

HP ScanJet 4p

The latest scanner from Hewlett-Packard is this low-cost color and grayscale model. The 4p is available in both Macintosh and Windows versions. Similar in appearance to the 4c, the 4p offers 300 ppi optical resolution and 1200 ppi interpolated resolution. It includes new HP PictureScan automatic scanning software. It also includes Visioneer PaperPort software, HP ScanJet Copy, Corel PHOTO-PAINT for Windows users, and Adobe Photoshop LE for Mac users. The 4p offers an ADF option, but does not offer a Transparency Adapter option.

OK, What Will It Do?

Now that you know what a scanner is and how one works, what can you do with yours? You are probably saying, "What a stupid question, does he think that I paid my hard-earned money and did not know what it would do?" Of course, I know that you know it scans! If you have used your scanner prior to reading this book, and if you have read the user guides, you already know some of the things you can do with your scanner. However, I have often found that new users purchased their scanners to do one particular thing and have never thought about some of the other things they can do with them. One of the reasons I had for writing this book was to showcase the many things you can do with an HP ScanJet scanner. Your scanner is a very versatile device. It is capable of scanning many different types of originals. You can even use it as a camera to scan 3-D objects. Following is just a sampling of what you can do with your ScanJet:

- **Scan Drawings and Line Art**
  Probably more scanners are used to scan this type of original than any other. Everyday, people scan company logos, cartoons, charts, drawings, illustrations, etc. This type of original is known as a drawing or line art and can be color or black-and-white. If you are producing a company, club, or church newsletter and are

printing on a laser printer or ink jet printer, this type of scanned image can be very effective.

■ **Scan Real 3-D Objects**
You can use your HP ScanJet color scanner as a camera (with limitations) to scan real, physical objects such as stamps, watches, jewelry, cloth, wood, etc. Some users of HP ScanJet scanners have produced catalogs using scans of real objects such as samples of cloth, stamps, etc.

See Page 185 for instructions on how to scan real objects.

■ **Scan Photographs**
Your HP ScanJet color scanner can scan both color photographs and black-and-white photographs (also known as continuous tone or grayscale). Everyone likes photographs. Photographs are reality. With today's 600 dpi laser and ink jet printers, you can print scanned photographs with a level of detail and clarity that was thought impossible only a few years past. It is now possible for you to use your HP ScanJet color scanner to produce high-quality publications such as magazines

and marketing pieces by sending your scanned images to a high-resolution printing device called an *imagesetter* and then to a commercial printing press.

■ **Scan for the Computer Screen**
The explosion of the Internet's World Wide Web and the growth of multimedia has created a tremendous demand for images that can be transmitted over phone lines or placed on a CD-ROM for display on the user's computer screen. In fact, if it were not for scanned photographs and drawings, Web pages and multimedia would probably not be what they are today. Your HP ScanJet color scanner is an excellent input device for the Web, presentations, and multimedia as you don't need to scan at a

billion pixels or millions of colors for display on a computer screen.

Refer to Chapter 7 for an explanation of scanning for the computer screen.

■ Scan Text

Your HP ScanJet scanner combined with OCR software gives you the capability of scanning text from books, letters, documents, etc. and then converting the resulting scanned image into text that your word processor can edit and save. This can save hours of retyping (and sore wrists as well). Your HP ScanJet scanner probably came with an OCR software program.

Chapter 3

How to Select an
Image Type

Introduction

Your HP ScanJet color scanner will scan practically anything. You can even scan real, physical, 3-D objects. You can scan drawings, sketches, clip art, and photographs. When you scan something with your color scanner, it must know the type of the original (image type) so that it uses the appropriate number of levels of gray or color as well as the appropriate resolution. Your HP ScanJet color scanner can scan six image types:

- Black-and-white drawing
- Color drawing
- Black-and-white halftone
- Color halftone
- Black-and-white photograph
- Color photograph

Your HP ScanJet color scanner's DeskScan II software comes with these six basic image types and also offers these types with sharpening (a software process used for improving out-of-focus or fuzzy photographs) and different levels of gray or color (16, 256 or millions of colors, for example). You can also create your own custom image types.

This chapter will provide a description of each image type, will include examples of each, and will show you how to select the image type that will best reproduce your original or give you the effect you desire. In addition, the chapter will provide tips and techniques for selecting an image type.

Black-and-White Drawings

Everyone knows what a drawing is! We have all drawn with pencils, pens, or crayons since kindergarten. But to your HP ScanJet scanner, a black-and-white drawing is a special image type…it is a 1-bit graphic. Meaning, if you scan something as a black-and-white drawing, each of the pixels will be either black or white. Images with only black-and-white pixels are called *bi-level bitmaps*. A scanned black-and-white drawing has a bit depth of 1.

Original drawings can be pencil sketches, CAD drawings, blueprints, *clip art,* etc. Graphic designers and artists refer to these types of drawings as *line art.* The originals consist only of black lines or filled areas and white lines or filled areas. The original drawing can be in color, but if you scan it as a black-and-white drawing, the colored areas will be converted to black only.

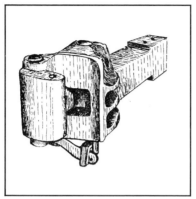

Historical drawing (circa 1911) scanned as a black-and-white drawing image type.

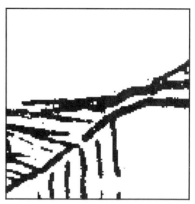

Same drawing scaled 1000%. Note there are only black or white pixels...no gray pixels.

Scanning a Photo as a Drawing

You can produce unusual and often dramatic effects by scanning a black-and-white or color photograph as a black-and-white drawing image type. This effect is sometimes called *thresholding*.

Scanned as a black-and-white photograph (256 levels of gray).

Same original photograph scanned as a black-and-white drawing.

Color Drawings

Most of what I wrote about black-and-white drawings also applies to color drawings. One of the image types supported by your ScanJet is color drawing. If your original is a color drawing, you may wish to use this image type.

When you use the color drawing image type, you have two options:

- Spot color
- Detailed

The choice of which to use will depend on the original drawing and the effect you desire. It is best to experiment and try both. Sometimes, you will get better results when scanning an original color drawing by using the color photo image type. Again, you should experiment to see which image type gives you the best results.

Black-and-White and Color Halftones

Halftones or halftoning is the process used for many years by newspapers and magazines to reproduce photographs using dots. black-and-white or color printing presses and desktop printers used with computers do not have infinite numbers of colors or shades of gray ink or toner to produce photographs on paper. The impression of continuous tone or color is produced by printing the photographic images with thousands of tiny dots (called halftone dots). Usually, these dots are all of the same size and the impression of tone or color is created by grouping these tiny dots into patterns.

Your HP ScanJet color scanner's DeskScan II software can scan your images using one of six halftone patterns. These halftone patterns are not needed if you are printing your scanned images on a printer that is capable of producing halftones. All Adobe PostScript and HP PCL printers have built-in halftoning capability. These halftones patterns are included in the DeskScan II software for those printers (such as dot matrix) that do not have built-in halftoning. You can use the DeskScan II halftone patterns on scanned images that will be printed on this type of printer, or you can use them to create a special effect.

HP DeskScan II software includes the following halftone patterns:

- Normal
- Fine
- Extra-fine
- Horizontal halftone
- Vertical line halftone
- Diffusion

Advantages and Disadvantages of Halftone Patterns

*T*he only real advantage of the halftone pattern is its smaller file size. I cannot recommend using the black-and-white or color halftones because of their several disadvantages.

Advantages

- The only advantage of using halftone patterns is the small files they produce. The files will be considerably smaller than grayscale or color images because color and grayscale images require a greater pixel depth and this creates larger files than do images scanned with halftone patterns.

Disadvantages

- You cannot edit an image scanned with a halftone pattern with an image editor, such as Adobe Photoshop.
- Halftoned images will produce moiré patterns (an undesirable screen pattern effect) and other artifacts when scaled (enlarged or reduced).
- Images that are scanned as halftone patterns do not display well on the computer screen and as a consequence, are almost useless for that purpose. This is because the computer screen has a lower resolution than the image and the dots will be very obvious. The exception is the diffusion pattern; this one works reasonably well for display on computer screens, but the black-and-white or color photo image type is better.

When using one of the halftone patterns, don't scan for the printer that you are using for proofing, scan for the one you intend to use for your final output.

Photograph vs. Halftone...A Comparison

The following example shows a photograph scanned as two different image types: a `Black-and-White Photo` and a `Black-and-White Halftone`. The halftone example doesn't reproduce well on a printing press because it is halftoned again by the imagesetter.

Black-and-White Photographs

*B*lack-and-white photography is not as popular as it once was. Color film and color photography have improved greatly in the past twenty years. Very few amateur photographers take black-and-white photographs and most professionals produce color because their customers demand it. It is sometimes difficult to find a place to have black-and-white film processed and printed. Most one-hour photo shops do not even accept black-and-white film so you are forced to look for a professional custom photo lab. Yet, a vast number of black-and-white photographs are still produced and an untold number exist in photo collections, in shoe boxes in attics, and in museums. You will surely scan a large number of black-and-white photographs with your HP ScanJet color scanner. Your ScanJet produces excellent black-and-white images.

16 or 256 Levels of Gray?

Your HP DeskScan II software image type options list photographs as black-and-white or color. Black-and-white photographs are also referred to as grayscale images. Your HP ScanJet can scan a black-and-white photograph as a 16-level grayscale (4-bit) or 256-level (8-bit) grayscale image. What is the difference and when should you use each? The following examples show the same photograph scanned as 16-level and 256-level grayscale. Note the greater shadow detail in the image on the right.

Scanned as a 16-level grayscale image.
File size: 90,254 bytes.

Scanned as a 256-level grayscale image. File size: 180,734 bytes.

The choice of 16 or 256 levels requires a tradeoff between file size and image quality. A 256-level scanned image will require more disk space to store an image than a 16-level image will (see the file sizes of the examples). The choice will also depend on what kind of photograph the original is. Does the original have a wide dynamic range; in other words, does it have many shades of gray or is it a high-contrast photograph with only a few shades of gray? If it is the latter, 16 levels of gray may be sufficient to accurately represent the original. If the original has a wide range of grays, 16 levels may produce an effect called *posterization*. You may also get a *banding effect* with 16 levels of gray in which the scanned image appears to have lines running across it.

Why Use Grayscale Instead of Haltone Patterns?

An image scanned using one of the halftone patterns will produce a smaller file, so why should you scan your photographs as grayscale instead of using one of the halftone patterns previously discussed? A grayscale image offers a number of advantages over the halftone pattern option:

■ Grayscale images can be edited with an image editor such as Adobe Photoshop or Corel PHOTO-PAINT. An image scanned as a halftone pattern can be edited with an image editor, but only with pixel editing tools such as pencils and erasers. You cannot make tone and color changes to halftoned images.

■ The contrast and brightness of a scanned grayscale or color image can be modified with an image editor or even with some desktop publishing programs.

Although the contrast and brightness of a scanned image can be changed after it has been scanned with an image editor or other program, you will get better results if you make these changes using DeskScan II. Any changes made to a scanned image result in some loss of data and perhaps detail.

- Grayscale images look better on the computer screen than images scanned with one of the halftoned patterns. If you are planning to use your black-and-white photographs on the Web or in multimedia presentations, scan them as grayscale (use the ScanJet `Black-and-White Photo` option and not the `Black-and-White Halftone` option).

- You can customize the line screen frequency (lines-per-inch) of grayscale images so that they will print optimally on different types of printers (see Page 102 for a description of line screen). A high-resolution printer will use a higher line screen frequency than a desktop printer and you will want your images to print well on both. You cannot change the line screen frequency of an image scanned with one of the halftone patterns.

- Grayscale images will be halftoned when they are printed using the halftone screen of a particular printer.

Color Photographs

We live in a colorful world. We watch color television and color movies. We read newspapers and magazines with color photographs. We take pictures of our families and vacation trips with color film in our cameras. Many of us regularly use the information super-highway (the Web or a commercial service such as America Online or CompuServe) to view color images and information provided in color. We all like color; it is realistic and pleasing to our eyes. Your HP ScanJet color scanner also "sees" in color and can scan color photographs (slides or prints) for printing or viewing on the computer screen.

16, 256, or Millions of Colors?

Your ScanJet color scanner can scan a color photo as a 4-bit image with 16 colors, an 8-bit image with 256 colors, or a 24-bit image with millions of colors. Which one should you use and why?

As when scanning black-and-white photographs, there is a tradeoff between image quality and file size when you have to choose between 16, 256, or millions of colors. It is true that a larger number of colors gives you better quality; but, how much quality do you need and how much disk space do you have? It is also important to consider what you are going to use the image for: displaying on the computer screen, printing on a 300 dpi desktop color printer, or outputting to a high-resolution 2500 dpi commercial printing press?

An important consideration in the 16, 256, or millions of colors decision is the original photograph. What type of image is it? Does it have wide range of colors? If the image has a limited range of colors, you may be able to produce a good scan using only 256 colors.

Color Photo Examples

The same 35 mm slide was scanned with 16, 256, and `Millions of Colors`. Each example is shown below with the file size that resulted. Refer to the Color Section to see these photographs in color.

If you are planning to use your images in high-quality publications that will be printed on a commercial printing press, you should scan the images with the `Millions of Colors` option. Using less than this could result in a posterization effect. If you are going to use your images for display only on the computer screen such as for the Web or for multimedia presentations, 256 colors can sometimes produce good results with most computer systems and the file sizes permit reasonable file download times.

Scanned with 16 colors. File size: 80,294 bytes.

Scanned with 256 colors. File size: 161,734 bytes (twice as large as the 16-color version).

Scanned with millions of colors. File size: 480,204 (six times as large as the 16-color version).

Chapter 4

EPSF
EPSF
EPSF (Screen Image)
MS Windows 3.0 Bitmap
OS/2 Bitmap
PCX
TIFF 5.0
TIFF 5.0 Compressed

BMP (*.BMP;*.RLE)
CompuServe GIF (*.GIF)
EPS (*.EPS)
JPEG (*.JPG)
PCX (*.PCX)
PICT File (*.PCT;*.PIC)

How to Select
a File Format

Introduction

So many file formats are used in the computer industry; there are well over one hundred in use at latest count. Choosing a file format can be intimidating to the beginner and confusing even to those who have used computers for years. Why are there so many formats and which ones should you use?

I am not sure if I understand why there are so many formats. Some of the reasons for the many formats are technical, some are financial, and some make no sense to me at all!

The HP DeskScan II software that accompanies your HP ScanJet color scanner gives you the option of saving your images in one of eight of the most popular file formats. It is likely that one of these file formats will satisfy most of your scanning requirements. In particular, TIFF and Encapsulated PostScript are the most widely used file formats and will probably serve your needs as well.

This chapter will explain the various file formats that are available directly when scanning with HP DeskScan II software and indirectly when using the TWAIN interface (TWAIN is explained and illustrated in Chapter 6). I will describe each of the file formats and will outline the advantages and disadvantages of each (most have both). The disk file space required for each file format will be shown by scanning an image and saving it in each of the formats.

Input and Output Considerations

*B*efore selecting a file format for your scanned images several factors must be considered. Some of these factors have to do with scanning the images and some with printing them. Consideration of these factors before you scan your images will keep you from using a format that will not work with your particular software or printer.

- What formats can I use with my computer?
- What formats are available when I use TWAIN?
- What formats can I use with the software programs (word processing, desktop publishing [DTP], etc.) that I will be using?
- What formats work with my printer?
- Will my scanned images be printed on a printing press by a commercial printer?

Macintosh and Windows Files

File compatibility between Apple Macintosh computers and PCs running Microsoft Windows has improved greatly since the early years of computer graphics and desktop publishing. Today, you can usually move a file successfully from one system to the other. There are differences between the way each system imports or reads files. Macintosh files include hidden attributes that let the Mac computer know the type of each file.

On the Windows side of the file conversion chasm, things are handled differently. Windows files do not include hidden attributes. Windows/DOS computers determine file attributes by reading the last three characters of a file name. This is called the *8 dot 3* system. Until Windows 95 and Windows NT, DOS and Windows files were limited to an eight-character name plus a three-character extension separated by a period (or dot). This three-character extension provides the file attributes to the application that is importing it. A TIFF file, for example, could have a name something like this: house.tif. Thus, Windows applications read the last three characters and determine that this is a TIFF file. If you are scanning an image on a Mac and know that it will be transferred to a PC running Windows, you should use the 8 dot 3 convention for your file names. Otherwise, the Windows software application will not know what type of file it is and may not be able to import it.

Which Formats Can I Use with my Computer?

Not all file formats are supported on both Apple Macintosh and Microsoft Windows computer systems. The following chart shows which HP ScanJet file formats can be used with Macintosh systems and which can be used with Windows computers:

File Format	Macintosh	Windows
TIFF	Supported	Supported
EPS (EPSF on the Mac)	Supported	Supported
PCX	Rarely Supported	Supported
PICT or PICT2	Supported	Rarely Supported
PICT Compressed	Supported	Not Supported
MacPaint	Supported	Not Supported
Windows Bitmap	Rarely Supported	Supported
OS/2 Bitmap	Not Supported	Supported

Some formats such as TIFF are available on both Macintosh and Windows systems. Some such as MacPaint are available on only one of the systems. If you are scanning an image that will be transferred from a Mac to a Windows PC (or vice versa), be sure to select a file format that is supported on both systems.

What Formats Can I Use with the Software Programs That I Will be Using?

Most software application programs support a limited number of the many file formats available. Before scanning an image for use in a program such as a word processor, image editor, or DTP program, be sure to determine which file formats the program accepts. Not all formats are supported by all applications. You can usually find this type of information in the documentation that accompanies the program (it may be in the online help), or you can start the program and use the file import or file load command. It will probably display a list of the acceptable formats.

Tip

If you have a difficult time determining what file formats a particular program accepts, or if you are scanning for an unknown program (you are sending the file to someone), use TIFF. TIFF is almost universally accepted by both Mac and Windows software programs.

What Formats Work with my Printer?

Most file formats will print on all types of printers. There is one major exception. Encapsulated PostScript (EPS or EPSF) files will not print well (or at all in some cases) on non-PostScript printers. If they print at all, they print a low-resolution 72 ppi image meant (usually a TIFF file) for displaying Encapsulated PostScript on computer screens. If you have a non-PostScript printer (usually Hewlett-Packard's PCL language is used, but there are others), don't save your scanned images as EPS or EPSF.

If your scanned images will be printed on a high-resolution imagesetter (such as an Agfa, Linotronic, or Montotype), the Encapsulated PostScript file format is an excellent choice, but you must print your proofs on a PostScript printer such as an HP LaserJet or HP DeskJet equipped with the PostScript option.

Will my Scanned Images be Printed on a Printing Press?

If your scanned images are destined to be printed by a commercial printer using a printing press, you should save your scanned images as TIFF or EPS files. These are the two most popular file formats and the ones that commercial printers have the most experience with. Some file formats will not be accepted at all by service bureaus or commercial printers. Be sure to consult with the service bureau or printer before taking or sending files to them.

See Chapter 11 for information on working with service bureaus and commercial printers.

TIFF

What Is TIFF?

TIFF is an abbreviation for *Tag Image File Format* and is the most widely used bitmapped graphical file format. TIFF was developed in 1986 specifically for scanned images by Aldus Corporation (now part of Adobe) and Microsoft. TIFF files may be 1-bit (bi-level), 4-, 8-, 24-, or 32-bit. TIFF files may be grayscale or color. The TIFF format supports both the red, green, blue (RGB) and cyan, magenta, yellow, black (CMYK) color models, but scanned images can only be of the RGB type. TIFF and TIFF compressed are two of the formats available to you when scanning with your HP ScanJet scanner. When used with Windows software programs, TIFF files have the MS-DOS three-character file extension: .TIF.

If there were one universal file format for graphics and scanned images it would be TIFF. It works with almost all applications on both Macintosh and Windows computers. It is available in both the Mac and Windows versions of DeskScan II. It works with practically every type of printer from dot matrix to high-resolution imagesetter. It is my recommendation for scanning images that will be printed.

Advantages of TIFF

- Most Macintosh and Windows software programs will import the TIFF format, either in the standard or compressed form (many programs support both). TIFF files are usually compatible between computer systems. Most of the time, a TIFF file produced with a Mac can be transferred to a PC running Microsoft Windows (see TIFF disadvantages below).

- TIFF images can be edited or modified by a number of paint programs or image editors. TIFF files can be compressed to save disk space, though not all application software can read compressed TIFF files.

- TIFF files can be changed by software applications that can import them. For example, a DTP program such as QuarkXpress has the capability to add color to a grayscale TIFF file before printing. Some applications, such as Adobe PageMaker, allow you to control the contrast, lightness or darkness, or other aspects of a TIFF file.

Disadvantages of TIFF

- The Macintosh and Windows versions of TIFF are very different. Fortunately, most Macintosh and Windows applications can import both types. If your application will not read a particular TIFF file, you may be able to convert it with an image editor such as Adobe Photoshop, or with a file conversion program such as HiJaak or DeBabelizer.

- There are several different variations or flavors of TIFF. Not all software applications fully or correctly implement the technical specification for the TIFF format. The TIFF files produced by your HP ScanJet color scanner should work with most applications. If they do not, you may be able to load them into an image editor such as Adobe Photoshop or Corel PHOTO-PAINT and save them with that program. Also, image conversion programs such as Quarterdeck's HiJaak can produce several versions of TIFF.

- TIFF files take longer to import into software applications than EPS/EPSF files because the application has to load the entire file before it can display the image on the computer screen. EPS/EPSF has a low-resolution preview header that is loaded before the rest of the file, resulting in faster load times for EPS/EPSF.

- Some software applications do not have the capability to separate color TIFF files. If you encounter this limitation, you can convert the file to EPS /EPSF with an image editor such as Adobe Photoshop.

Encapsulated PostScript (EPS/EPSF)

What Is EPS/EPSF?

PostScript was developed by Adobe Inc. in 1984 for use with the original Apple Macintosh and Apple Laserwriter printer. Most experts in the computer industry date the beginning of computer publishing and desk-top publishing with the introduction of the PostScript language. PostScript is a special type of computer language called a *page description language*. PostScript was developed specifically for printing text and graphical images on color and black-and-white printers such as laser printers, inkjet printers, and high-resolution imagesetters. Encapsulated PostScript is a special version of the PostScript developed for vector graphic files and bitmapped graphics including scanned images. When using a Macintosh, Encapsulated PostScript files are abbreviated EPSF. When using a Windows computer, they are abbreviated EPS and they have the MS-DOS three-character file extension: .EPS.

Advantages of EPS/EPSF

- Encapsulated PostScript is normally thought of as a vector graphic format (see Chapter 8), but an EPS/EPSF file can also include bitmapped graphics such as scanned images.

- The PostScript language and Encapsulated PostScript files are standards within the graphics and publishing worlds. EPS/EPSF is used on both Macintosh and Windows computers and can even be transferred to mini-computers and workstations.

- EPS/EPSF files can be saved in standard ASCII text format as well as binary format codes. If they are saved as ASCII, they can be edited with a word processor or text editor, but this is not recommended.

■ With EPS/EPSF, you can save image editor clipping paths and halftoning information. Clipping paths allow you to mask part of an image so that the image stands out from a white background. You should only include halftoning information with your EPS/EPSF files if you understand the techniques of halftoning or have consulted with your commercial printer.

■ The EPS/EPSF format supports 24-bit RGB files or 32-bit CMYK files.

Disadvantages of EPS/EPSF

■ The greatest disadvantage of the EPS/EPSF format is that the files must be printed on a PostScript printer. If you attempt to print an EPS/EPSF file on a non-PostScript printer, it will either not print at all, or the low-resolution PICT or TIFF header preview file will be printed (something you probably don't want as the preview headers usually have a resolution of about 72 ppi).

■ The second disadvantage of the EPS/EPSF format is that the files do not directly display on your computer screen. EPS/EPSF files can only be displayed by high-end UNIX workstations equipped with special display software called *Display PostScript*. Macintosh and Windows computers get around this limitation by use of a preview header. This is a low-resolution PICT (Macintosh) or TIFF (Windows) file that is attached to the EPS/EPSF file. When you import an EPS/EPSF file into an application, this low-resolution header preview file is displayed on your computer screen. Only a few software applications (primarily image editors like Adobe Photoshop can directly view EPS/EPSF files).

When you save a scanned image as an EPS/EPSF file with HP DeskScan II software you can save the file with or without the Macintosh PICT preview header or the Windows TIFF preview header. These preview header files make the EPS/EPSF file size larger. If you save EPS/EPSF files without the preview header, you will not be able to see a preview of your scanned image when you import it into software applications. On the Macintosh you will see a box containing text about the file. On a Windows system, you will see a box with a large X.

■ The third disadvantage of the EPS/EPSF format is that files are twice as large (disk space) as other formats such as TIFF.

■ Finally, not all software applications support the EPS/EPSF format. Many can import EPS/EPSF files, but cannot create or export them. Some image editors cannot import EPS/EPSF files.

The two image editors included with current HP ScanJet scanners (Adobe Photoshop on the Mac and Corel PHOTO-PAINT on Windows) can import EPS/EPSF files.

MacPaint

What Is MacPaint?

MacPaint was one of the first painting file formats developed for the original Apple Macintosh computer. It takes its name from the MacPaint image editing program. MacPaint was developed to be the format for the MacPaint program and was intended to be a simple file format for computers with limited amounts of RAM and disk space.

Advantages of MacPaint

- The MacPaint format was previously supported by most Macintosh software programs, but is not as widely used today.

Disadvantages of MacPaint

- MacPaint files can have a maximum resolution of 72 ppi.
- MacPaint files can have a maximum image size of 720 x 576 pixels. If you scan an image larger than 720 x 576 pixels, part of the image will automatically be cropped off.
- MacPaint scanned images can only be black-and-white drawings or black-and-white halftones (1-bit black and white images). MacPaint scanned images cannot be a black-and-white or color photograph or color drawing.
- Most Windows software applications cannot import MacPaint files. If you plan to exchange files between a Mac and Windows PC, do not use the MacPaint format.

PICT

What Is PICT?

PICT is an abbreviation of the PICTure file format. PICT was one of the first graphical file formats for the original Macintosh computer in 1984. PICT files can be either a vector graphic or a bitmapped image. Your HP ScanJet color scanner uses an upgraded, more advanced version of PICT called PICT2. When used with Windows or MS-DOS software programs, PICT files have the MS-DOS three-character file extension: .PCT.

Advantages of PICT

- PICT files may be either bitmaps or vector images. Images scanned with your HP ScanJet are always bitmaps.
- The PICT format imposes no limitations on image resolution.
- PICT supports RLE and JPEG file compression.
- PICT2 files may contain up to 16.7 million colors in the 24-bit RGB form.
- PICT is the file format used by the Macintosh clipboard.
- Almost all Macintosh programs will import PICT images.
- PICT is the primary file format for Apple Macintosh multimedia authoring programs such as Macromedia Director (it is the default file format for the Mac version of Director).

Disadvantages of PICT

- The PICT format is not supported by the Windows version of HP DeskScan II.
- The image controls in many Macintosh programs, such as contrast and brightness, may not work with PICT files.
- PICT is not as widely supported by Windows software as other formats such as TIFF or EPS/EPSF.
- PICT is not widely accepted by service bureaus and commercial printers; in fact, many refuse to accept the file format at all.

PICT Compressed

What Is PICT Compressed?

PICT Compressed is a special version of PICT that uses Apple's Quick-Time software and that allows you to save PICT files in several different compressed formats. Each of these formats offers different levels of image quality, compression ratios, and support by other software programs (such as DTPs, word processors, etc.). These formats include:

- (Apple) Animation
- Compact Video
- Component Video
- (PICT) Graphics
- (PICT) None

- (PICT) Photo–JPEG
- (PICT) Video

Apple's QuickTime software must be installed to use most of the PICT compressed formats.

PCX

What Is PCX?

PCX is an abbreviation of PC Paintbrush. This file format is one of the oldest graphical file formats. It was developed by ZSoft as the format of its PC Paintbrush software. PCX files have the MS-DOS three-character file extension: .PCX.

Advantages of PCX

- Almost all Windows and MS-DOS software programs will import PCX.

Disadvantages of PCX

- PCX was developed for MS-DOS systems and not all Macintosh programs will import PCX files.
- Most service bureaus or commercial printers will not accept PCX files.
- There are several versions of the PCX format and you may encounter compatibility problems.

Windows Bitmap

What Is Windows Bitmap?

This format was developed by Microsoft. It is the default bitmapped graphics file format for Microsoft Windows and Microsoft application programs. Windows Bitmap files have the MS-DOS three-character file extension: .BMP.

Advantages of Windows Bitmap

- Windows Bitmap is the standard file format for Microsoft Windows. It is widely supported by Windows software applications.

- Windows bitmaps can be black-and-white (1-bit), grayscale, 4-bit, 8-bit, 24-bit, or 32-bit color.

- The Windows Bitmap format is now widely used by Microsoft Windows multimedia authoring programs such as Macromedia Director (it is the default file format for the Windows version of Director).

Disadvantages of Windows Bitmap

- The Windows Bitmap format is almost exclusively used on Windows PCs. It cannot be used on the Apple Macintosh.

- This format does not have good file compression. It does not do a good job of compressing 24-bit images.

- This format is seldom used by service bureaus or commercial printers. In fact, some will refuse to accept this format. If you are planning to send your work to a service bureau or commercial printer, you should consider using TIFF or EPS/EPSF instead of BMP.

OS/2 Bitmap

What Is OS/2 Bitmap?

The OS/2 Bitmap format is for use with the OS/2 operating system and OS/2 software applications. OS/2 Bitmap files have the MS-DOS three-character file extension: .BMP.

Advantages of OS/2 Bitmap

- This format is the standard default bitmapped graphics file format for OS/2. Scanned images can be saved in the OS/2 bitmap format as any of the DeskScan II image types. OS/2 bitmaps can be 1-bit, 4-bit, 8-bit, or 24-bit color.

- OS/2 bitmaps are widely supported by OS/2 software applications.

Disadvantages of OS/2 Bitmap

- As with the Windows Bitmap format, this format cannot be used with an Apple Macintosh. It is not widely supported by Windows software applications.

- As with the Windows Bitmap format, this format does not have good file compression. It does not do a good job of compressing 24-bit images.

- As with Windows Bitmaps, this format is seldom used by services bureaus or commercial printers. In fact, some will refuse to accept this format. If you are planning to send your work to a service bureau or commercial printer, save the image as a TIFF or EPS/EPSF file.

File Size

A major factor in selecting a file format for your scanned images is how much disk space each format requires. To illustrate the disk space requirements of each format supported by HP ScanJet color scanners, I scanned a black-and-white photograph (grayscale), a black-and-white drawing (line art), and a color photograph. I saved each example in all of the HP ScanJet file formats supported. I used the default settings for each scan and the only variation was the file format. A chart follows each set of examples showing the file sizes of each format.

The charts show that Encapsulated PostScript with a screen image requires the most disk space of all the file formats. It requires approximately 11 times as much disk storage space as the PICT format (which requires the least amount of disk space except for MacPaint which has a maximum resolution of 72 ppi).

Black-and-White Photograph Example

The black-and-white photo shown below was scanned as a 256-level, grayscale, 150-ppi image in each of the file formats supported by your HP ScanJet (the MacPaint format is 72 ppi and, due to the limitations of that format, part of the image was cropped). The chart shows how much disk space was required to scan this image in each of the file formats.

File Format Disk Space Requirements

File Format	File Size (bytes)
TIFF 5.0	239,486
TIFF 5.0 Compressed	234,226
Encapsulated PostScript	509,277
Encapsulated PostScript (with screen image)	529,125
Windows Bitmap	241,320
0S/2 Bitmap	241,036
PCX	307,073
MacPaint (scanned at 72 ppi)	78,825
PICT	243,720

Black-and-White Drawing Example

The following line art example was scanned with the DeskScan II `Black-and-White Drawing` option at 600 ppi in each of the file formats supported by your HP ScanJet scanner (the MacPaint format was scanned at 72 ppi and part of the image was cropped due to limitations of the format). The following chart shows how much disk space was required to scan this image in each of the file formats.

File Format Disk Space Requirements

File Format	File Size (bytes)
TIFF 5.0	445,570
TIFF 5.0 Compressed	441,223
Encapsulated PostScript	920,190
Encapsulated PostScript (with screen image)	926,953
Windows Bitmap	448,448
0S/2 Bitmap	448,480
PCX	137,089
MacPaint (scanned at 72 ppi)	148,500
PICT	123,112

Color Photo Example

The following color photograph was scanned with the DeskScan II `Sharp Color Photograph` option at 200 ppi in each of the file formats supported by your HP ScanJet scanner (the MacPaint format was scanned at 72 ppi and part of the image was cropped due to limitations of the format). The chart shows how much disk space was required to scan this image in each of the file formats.

To see this photograph in color, refer to Figure 18 in the Color Section.

File Format Disk Space Requirements

File Format	File Size (bytes)
TIFF 5.0	1,148,628
TIFF 5.0 Compressed	1,294,586
Encapsulated PostScript	2,328,856
Encapsulated PostScript (with screen image)	2,594,198
Windows Bitmap	1,150,374
0S/2 Bitmap	1,150,090
PCX	1,360,323
MacPaint (scanned at 72 dpi)	52,686
PICT	201,434

Converting File Formats

If your word processing, desktop publishing, or other application does not support the file format you wish to use with your HP ScanJet, it may be possible to convert the scanned image file to a different format. Bitmap paint programs and image editors allow you to import images in one format and save them as a different format. Several file conversion programs are available for both Macintosh and MS-DOS systems that can convert a bitmapped image in one format to a different bitmapped format (TIFF to PCX, for example).

To convert a bitmapped image to a vector image, you must trace the bitmapped image with a tracing program or illustration program with tracing capabilities.

Refer to Chapter 6 for an explanation of the tracing process.

Using the Clipboard for File Conversions

The Macintosh and Microsoft Windows clipboards also offer additional file format conversion possibilities. If your application software does not import any of the DeskScan II file formats or your image editor formats, you may be able to cut or copy a graphic to the clipboard, paste it into the application, and save it in a format that your software supports.

Example of Using the Clipboard with DeskScan II Software and a Word Processor

1. Start DeskScan II. Click the **Preview** button. Make any desired adjustments with the DeskScan II controls.

2. Click on **Edit** in the DeskScan II menu bar.

3. Select **Copy**.

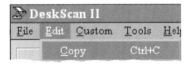

4. DeskScan II will scan the part of the image that you select to the Windows or Macintosh clipboard.

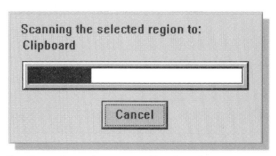

5. Start the software application that you want to put the image into.

6. Use the application's **Paste** command to insert the image.

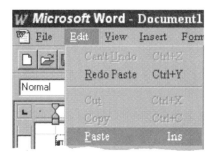

More File Formats with TWAIN

*S*ometimes you may find that you need to use a file format that is not one of those supported by your HP ScanJet. You may, for example, wish to upload a scanned image to one of the online services such as CompuServe or the Internet. The most common file formats for the Internet's World Wide Web, computer Bulletin Board Services (BBSs), and commercial online services are GIF and JPEG (a new file format, PNG, has been developed to replace GIF). GIF and JPEG are not supported by the HP ScanJet scanner. So, how do you get your scanned images into the GIF or JPEG formats? Use TWAIN!

What File Formats are Available with TWAIN?

So many file formats are available through applications that support TWAIN that it is not possible to describe all of them here. The following table lists some of the file formats that are not supported directly by the HP DeskScan II software, but can be used through TWAIN.

File Format	Macintosh	Windows
JPEG	Supported	Supported
GIF	Supported	Supported
CGM	Supported	Supported
GEM	Not Supported	Supported
Targa Bitmap (TGA)	Supported	Supported
Scitex CT Bitmap	Supported	Supported
Windows Metafile (WMF)	Not Supported	Supported
Kodak Photo CD (PCD)	Supported	Supported
PNG	Supported	Supported
FlashPix (FPX)	Supported	Supported

JPEG

JPEG is an abbreviation of *Joint Photographic Experts Group*, commonly pronounced "jay peg." Both Macintosh and Windows applications support JPEG. When used on a PC running Windows, JPEG files have the MS-DOS three-character extension: .JPG

Advantages of JPEG

- JPEG can significantly decrease the file size of a scanned image.
- JPEG has become one of the predominant graphic standards for online services such as the World Wide Web on the Internet (the other standard is the GIF file format, which will be replaced by PNG).

Disadvantages of JPEG

- JPEG uses *lossy* compression, which means the compressed file has lost some data (meaning it has lost some quality). How much quality is lost and whether it is noticeable by the average person depends on how much the file is compressed.

- Software application programs occasionally implement JPEG differently and you may encounter compatibility problems.

- Repeatedly compressing and decompressing JPEG files can significantly degrade the quality of images.

Save your scanned images in another format, then use JPEG on a copy of the file.

JPEG Options

When you use an image editor such as Adobe Photoshop to save an image as a JPEG file, you are given several options that control the amount of file compression and thus the quality of the image. The degree to which the image quality is degraded depends on the amount of compression. File compression and image quality are always compromises. If you go too far with compression, your image quality will suffer.

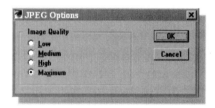

The Adobe Photoshop JPEG options. You can choose between low or maximum image quality. Low image quality gives you small files and maximum quality produces the largest files.

JPEG Examples

Following are examples that show the file sizes that result by changing the image quality setting of JPEG compression. The example is a 35mm slide scanned with the HP ScanJet Transparency Adapter at 300 ppi. The image was saved as three JPEG files with a different quality level for each file. You can see these same files in color in the Color Section.

Scanned as a TIFF file at 300 ppi. File size is 1,675,924 bytes.

Saved as a JPEG file with low quality. File size is 118,998 bytes.

Saved as a JPEG file with medium quality. File size is 170, 640 bytes.

Saved as a JPEG file with maximum quality. File size is 628,804 bytes.

GIF

GIF is an abbreviation for *Graphics Interchange Format* which is commonly pronounced "jiff" or "giff." GIF was made popular by the CompuServe online information service and it has rapidly become the file format of choice for online services including World Wide Web pages on the Internet.

GIF is supported by both Macintosh and Windows systems and applications. When used on a PC running Windows, GIF files have the MS-DOS three character extension: .GIF.

Advantages of GIF

- GIF files are one of the most compact file formats, making them ideal for use online and for file transfer. GIF files are low-resolution and limited to 8-bit color images (see the disadvantages below).

- GIF files are automatically compressed using LZW compression.

- GIF compression is lossless, meaning you do not lose image quality.

- You can create animations with the GIF format by including a number of images in one file. The multiple images in the GIF files are displayed rapidly in succession creating the impression of movement.

Disadvantages of GIF

- The GIF format is limited to 8-bit indexed colors, meaning that GIF files can contain a maximum of 256 colors.

- Most DTP and word processing programs cannot import GIF files.

- There are several versions of GIF and not all online services and Web browsers support both.

- The Unisys Corporation, who developed the GIF file compression algorithm (called "LZW"), has begun to enforce patent rights. Unisys is charging a license fee to any software company that creates or writes a GIF file. A new file format has been developed by the online community to replace GIF and eliminate these licensing fees and concerns. This new file format is called the Portable Network Graphics (PNG) format (see Page 59).

The GIF format comes in two major versions: GIF87a and GIF89a. The GIF89a version was developed to permit transparent colors and to add interlacing. These two features were greatly desired by graphic artists and illustrators who were designing graphics for online services and especially for the World Wide Web. Transparent colors let you create images that appear to be directly on the background. Interlacing is a method of storing the pixels in a GIF file that can be utilized by Web browsers and GIF viewers to quickly display a low-resolution image and then gradually become sharper. If you have used the Web or a service like CompuServe, you have probably observed this. The weather maps on CompuServe are GIF files that display this way.

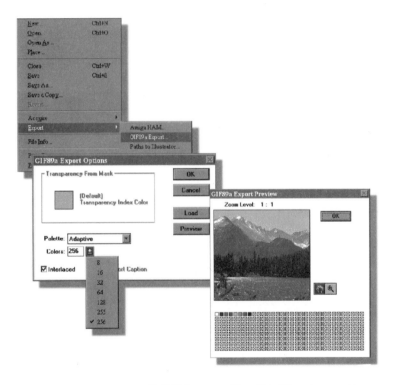

The Adobe Photoshop 3 GIF89a export filter. This filter gives you the options of designating a color to be transparent, a choice of palettes, the number of colors, and the option to interlace the file.

GIF Examples

Following are examples that show the file sizes that result by changing the number of colors. The example is a 35mm slide scanned with the HP ScanJet Transparency Adapter at 250 ppi. The image was exported as three GIF files with 8, 64, and 256 colors using Adobe Photoshop's GIF89a filter. These same images may be seen in color in the Color Section.

Scanned at 250 ppi and saved as a TIFF file. File size is 750,494 bytes.

Indexed color image exported with Photoshop's GIF89a filter using eight colors. File size is 52,732.

Indexed color image exported with the GIF89a filter using 64 colors. File size is 143,875.

Indexed color image exported with the GIF89a filter using 256 colors. File size is 190,886.

PNG

PNG is an abbreviation of *Portable Network Graphics* and is pronounced "ping." PNG was developed to overcome the legal problems with GIF and at the same time to produce a file format that was superior to GIF.

PNG is supported by both Macintosh and Windows systems and applications. When used on a PC running Windows, PNG files have the MS-DOS three character extension: .PNG.

Advantages of PNG

- The PNG file format is not limited to 8-bit indexed color as is GIF. PNG supports up to 16-bit (grayscale) and 48-bit color pixel depth, meaning that your images can have up to trillions of colors (your HP ScanJet color scanner does not support 48-bit color).

- PNG uses the ZIP file compression method (the same method as used by the well-known Pkzip program). ZIP is royalty-free, meaning that you or anyone who uses ZIP does not have to pay a fee to use the compression method. ZIP is a "lossless" compression method, meaning that image quality does not degrade after compression.

- PNG supports alpha channels used by image editors such as Adobe Photoshop and Corel PHOTO-PAINT. Alpha channels are used to produce transparent effects in images. The GIF format supports only one level of transparency, but PNG supports multiple transparent levels.

- PNG uses a 2D interlacing method, whereas GIF uses a linear interlacing method (interlacing is the technique used to progressively display images being downloaded from the Web or other online service). The GIF interlacing method progressively displays images and appears as though a windowshade is being pulled down. The PNG method displays a full image that is blurred at first, but becomes gradually sharper as more of the file is downloaded.

Disadvantages of PNG

- PNG does not support multiple images in one file (you cannot do animations with PNG files).

- The PNG format was not widely supported by software applications at the time this book was going to press.

I cannot show you an example of a PNG file as the program I used to produce this book (Corel Ventura Publisher 5.0) does not support PNG and I could not import PNG images.

Chapter 5

How to Get the
Best Color Scan

Introduction

Assume you you have installed your HP ScanJet color scanner. You faithfully read the user documentation that accompanied the scanner (you did read it, didn't you?). You have scanned some images and have impressed your friends and family. You have a suspicion that you are not getting the best scans that you could. You also have a feeling that your scanned images could look better. This chapter is intended to show you how to use your HP DeskScan II software to get the optimal results from your HP ScanJet scanner. I have tried not to duplicate the information provided in the user guides (I hate books that warm over the product's user guides). I have tried to give you tips and suggestions that will enable you to use the tools more effectively and to explain the strengths (and limitations) of the tools. The first step is to start at the beginning (profound thought, huh?).

Start with *Good Originals*

Your HP ScanJet color scanner combined with powerful image editing software is capable of producing some truly amazing results. This combination can often be used to save photographs that seemed destined for the trash can. With the controls and tools in the Deskscan II software or one of the image editors, you can correct mistakes that were made during the shooting of the photograph or in the darkroom during processing or printing. Sometimes photographs that have been damaged can be restored.

Now, having said all that, let me emphasize that to produce the best possible results with your HP ScanJet color scanner, you should start the process with the best possible original! The HP ScanJet scanner is a remarkable example of technology. It can, when combined with patience and time, seem to work wonders. The key words are: patience and time. Image editing can be time-consuming and can require a degree of patience. Depending on how poor the original or how great the damage, the process may require more than you are willing to expend. For some, image editing is a very creative, satisfying experience. For others, it can be painful. Having the best possible original can either eliminate the need for image editing or reduce it to an acceptable level.

Good, Bad, and Ugly Photographs

It is not possible in this text to list all of the attributes of a good photograph. Good photography is a mixture of art and science and professionals have been debating the properties of good photography for over a century. It is possible, however, to describe a few of the major attributes of good photography and of bad photographs. The following are some guidelines of things to look for and to avoid:

What Makes a Good Photograph?

A wise person (I don't remember who) once said that "beauty is in the eye of the beholder." Serious photographers, when they aren't arguing about cameras and film, debate endlessly about what is (and is not) a good photograph. It is easier to define the technical attributes of good photography than the artistic attributes. What is important here is to know what your HP ScanJet scanner can do (and cannot do) when scanning a photograph or drawing. The old proverb of "garbage in, garbage out" also applies to scanning. The following list of the technical attributes of a good photograph is provided so that you will have a better understanding of the possibilities and limitations of scanning with your HP ScanJet color scanner.

- **Photographs with normal exposure**
  With today's automatic exposure cameras, poorly exposed negatives or slides are not as common as they once were. A good photo lab can correct for incorrect exposure to a certain extent. Especially when working with black-and-white photographs, there is much a lab can do to produce a good print from negatives that are not perfect. This is less true with color negatives or slides. The exposure latitude of a slide is less than any other type of film and the photo lab has no options for correcting exposure when processing slide film. You should try to get the best possible print from a negative for scanning. Your HP ScanJet scanner can correct for a print that is too dark or too light to a point. DeskScan's automatic exposure control takes care of most situations. You can also use the DeskScan II controls to make manual adjustments. But, there are limitations to what the software can do and it may be better to have a new print made rather than to spend a lot of time trying to adjust the controls.

■ **Photographs with normal contrast**

Contrast is the range of tones and colors between dark and light. A photograph can have a wide range or narrow range. The range can be too narrow (photographers call this "flat") or too wide (high-contrast). This is not to imply that you would never want a high-contrast photograph. Sometimes this is the effect you want. It means that if it were not the effect you wanted, you would have to do some work with DeskScan II or your image editor to correct it.

This photograph (Crescent Lake in Washington state) has normal contrast. There is an even distribution of tones from light to dark.

This photograph has low contrast...shadows are too light...not enough tonal range. Someone in London has a sense of humor!

This photograph (Boyd Lake in Colorado) has high contrast. Technically, this is not a good photograph, but it works artistically.

Attempting to produce a wider range of tones does not work in this case. You cannot bring out detail that is not in the original negative.

What Makes a Bad Photograph?

The following list is not intended to define the artistic attributes of a bad photograph. It is a list of photographic defects or problems that you should avoid (if possible) when selecting photographs to scan. I know that it is not always possible to avoid photographs with these defects…you may want to scan them to correct these defects! I am saying that starting with a good photograph will make the scanning process easier and it will go faster if you have good originals to begin with.

- **Out-of-focus or unsharp photos**
  Most of the time, this is caused by camera shake or movement rather than poor focus. Although both HP DeskScan II and most image editing software offer a sharpening feature, there are limitations to what the software can do without creating artifacts.

- **Cracked or damaged photographs**
  Photographic prints that have cracks in the emulsion or that have other physical damage can often be saved by using an image editor. However, this is time-consuming and can be tedious. If you have access to the negative, it would be easier and quicker to have a new print made.

- **Stained or soiled photographs**
  I know it is hard to believe, but some people do not take good care of their precious photographs. Sometimes they are actually careless enough to spill coffee, tea, or milk on them! In over twenty years as a professional photographer, I have been asked to fix photographs with the weirdest things on them. The same suggestion that I made about cracked photos applies to stained ones. If you have access to the negative, have a new print made. It is possible to use your image editor to retouch the photo to remove the stain, but it can be time-consuming.

A technique I used many times during my photography career may be useful. Place a sheet of transparent film or acetate that is the same color as the stain on top of the photograph before you scan it. You can obtain this type of material at a camera store or artist's supply shop. Because the material is the same color as the stain, the stain will not show when scanned. This technique works well with black-and-white photographs, but not as well with color photos.

Good, Bad, and Ugly Drawings

Some of the things that make a photograph bad can also make a drawing a bad choice for scanning. Drawings are also called *line art* and can include drawings produced by hand with a pen or pencil, sketches, blueprints, or technical illustrations produced by hand or with a computer. The following list is intended to be a guide in selecting drawings for scanning. I realize that sometimes you cannot avoid selecting a drawing that may not be perfect. Some historical drawings have not survived well. Perhaps they were not stored under ideal conditions or were mishandled. You may have no other option than to try to get the best scan you can. These recommendations are intended to minimize the amount of image editing and retouching that you will have to do.

- Try to avoid drawings or line art that have physical damage such as cracks or tears in the paper. Sometimes it is possible to use an image editor to remove evidence of cracks or tears. If the crack or tear goes across a part of the image the task will be more difficult…I didn't say impossible, I just said it might be difficult or time-consuming.

- Try to avoid drawings that are stained, discolored, or faded. Again, I know this may be impossible. The drawing may be the only one available (or even the only one in existence) and you may have no other option (see the previous page for a tip on how to remove stains from scans). Another option for fixing drawings that are stained or discolored is to scan the drawing then trace it with a tracing or drawing program.

Refer to Chapter 8 for an explanation of the tracing process.

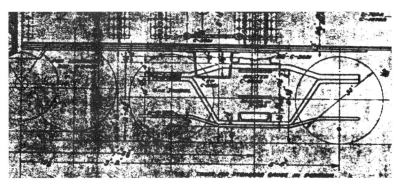

Sometimes it is hopeless! This drawing was in such bad shape that nothing I attempted with DeskScan II or even an image editor could save it. It had been repeatedly copied and the resulting discoloration could not be removed because it is the same color as the lines of the drawing.

Highlights, Middle Tones, and Shadows

To effectively use the controls and tools in the DeskScan II software to modify, correct, or enhance color or grayscale photographs, you need to understand and recognize the highlights, shadows, and middle tones that exist in photographs. Most correctly exposed photographs have a full range of tones. These range from dark (shadows) through middle tones to light (highlights). Some high-contrast photographs, such as sunset scenes, may not have many, if any, middle tones; but, typical photographs have the full range of tones.

When I say "correctly exposed" photographs, I am not only referring to the action that takes place in the camera, I also mean anything that happens during processing and printing in the darkroom. A photograph can be correctly exposed in the camera and incorrectly exposed in the darkroom.

The following photograph illustrates what shadows, highlights, and middle tones look like in a normally exposed and processed photograph:

■ *Shadows* are the darkest part of the photograph (in some photos, the shadows will have no detail and are pure black).

■ *Highlights* are the lightest part of the photograph (in a normal photo these areas should have some detail and rarely be all white).

■ *Middle tones* should range in tone and color somewhere between the highlights and shadows.

Lighting Conditions for Color Viewing

*T*o produce good color with your HP ScanJet color scanner, you need to have good lighting conditions for your monitor and for the prints from your color printer. Your monitor should be placed so that there is no glare on the screen. It may be necessary to move the monitor or to move portable lighting to create a glare-free environment. If permanent lighting is causing the problem, you may have to put a hood over your monitor to shield it from the light. Commercial hoods for computer monitors are available, or you can make one by cutting cardboard and attaching it to your monitor with Velcro or tape.

You also need to be aware of your monitor's surroundings. Large areas of bright colors such as walls, drapes, etc. can influence your perception of color on your monitor. It may be impossible to do anything about the walls or drapes, but if you can, place your monitor in an area with neutral color (gray is best, but white will work also).

Color Monitor Calibration

*Y*our HP DeskScan II software includes a monitor calibration program. You cannot correctly judge color if your computer monitor's contrast and brightness are incorrectly set. After your monitor is calibrated, it may look different from what you are accustomed to. Don't panic and change it back too quickly. Give it a chance to grow on you. Use the new calibration with DeskScan II and with your image editor. You may notice that you are getting better scans sooner with fewer printouts.

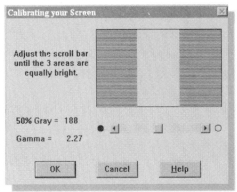

HP DeskScan II monitor calibration. Refer to your HP Scan-Jet User Guide for instructions.

Calibrating Your HP ScanJet Color Scanner

*T*o get the best possible color or grayscale scan for printing, your HP ScanJet color scanner needs to know what printer and software you will be using to print the image (or view it on a computer screen). HP does this with a process it calls *print path calibration*. A print path contains information about the printer and software application that you will use to produce your final output.

Print Path Calibration Process

Each desktop printer and commercial printing press has individual characteristics that must be taken into account to produce a scan that prints best on the particular printer. Both desktop printers and commercial printing presses have halftoning processes and these processes are not the same between brands and models of printers, or even among printers from the the same brand and model. HP includes pre-built calibration paths for the most popular models of Hewlett-Packard black-and-white and color printers, as well as a Linotronic imagesetter used in commercial printing. You can use these print path calibrations to get started, but I highly recommend that you take the time to produce a print path for your own individual printer. It is especially critical to do this if you plan to produce your final output on a commercial color printing press.

Scanned with the wrong print path calibration for the printer being used.

Scanned with the correct print path calibration for the printer being used.

Some software application programs such as Adobe Photoshop, Quark-Xpress, and Corel PHOTO-PAINT include their own halftoning methods and processes that can override the halftoning built into the printer. If your final output is to a commercial printing press, your printer will use special software called *color separation software* to produce printing plates from your images. Your HP ScanJet color scanner needs to know about the halftoning characteristics of the particular applications that you will be using for your final output. The HP DeskScan II print path calibration process includes the capability of including a calibration target in your software application and of producing a print path when you print this target from the application.

The process uses two calibration targets, one color and the other 256 levels of gray. This target is printed on the printer used for your final output. The printed target is then scanned on your HP ScanJet and a print path calibration is automatically created by DeskScan.

Creating a Print Path Calibration for Your Desktop Printer

1. Click on **Custom** in the DeskScan II menu.

2. Click on **Print Path** in the **Custom** menu.

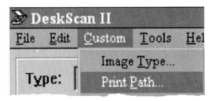

3. Click on **New...**

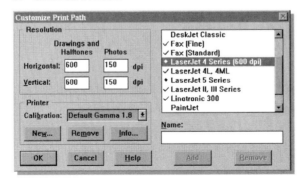

4. Click on **Create...**

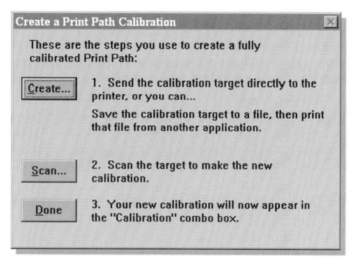

5. Click on the **Printer** button in the Send To area.

6. Click on **Black and White** or **Color** in the Printer Information area. Type the normal resolution of the printer in the Native Printer Resolution box.

7. Click on **OK**. A calibration target will be sent to your printer from DeskScan. Use the same printer that you will use for your final output.

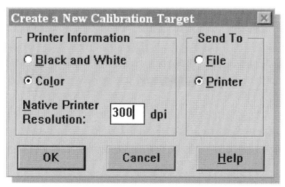

8. The calibration target will print on your selected printer.

New printer toner cartridges print darker than ones that have been used a bit, so do not use a new printer toner cartridge when printing your print path calibration targets. If you have no choice but to use a new cartridge, print 50 to 100 pages on your printer before printing the target. This will stabilize the print cartridge and produce normal print levels.

9. Repeat Steps 1 — 3.

10. Click on **Scan...**

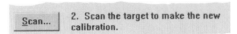

11. Place the target that you just printed on the scanner glass. Align it with the top and right side of the scanner glass. Carefully close the scanner lid and click on **OK**.

12. Type a name for the calibration path (suggestion: use the name of your printer; e.g., `deskjet1600`).

13. Click on **Save**.

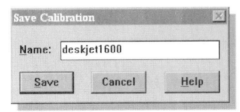

14. Click on **Done**. The new calibration will now be available for use any time that you scan an image that will be printed with that printer.

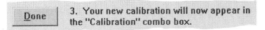

Use the same type of paper to print your calibration target that you will be using for your normal output.

For information on selecting papers for printing scanned images, see Page 199.

Creating a Print Path Calibration for Your Software Applications

1. Click on **Custom** in the DeskScan II menu.

2. Click on **Print Path** in the **Custom** menu.

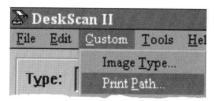

3. Click on **New ...** in the `Printer` area.

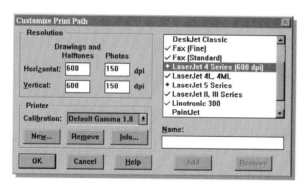

4. Click on **Create...**

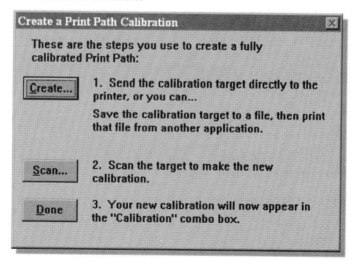

5. Click on the **File** button in the `Send To` area. This creates a
calibration target file that can be imported into the application you
plan to use for your final output.

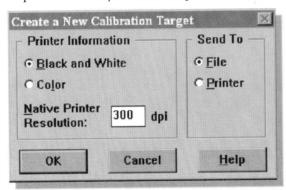

6. To save the Black and White calibration target, click the arrow to the
right of `Save as type:` Click on one of the file types (use the same
file type you will be using for your scanned images). Type a name for
the Black and White calibration file in the `File name:` box. Click
on **Save**.

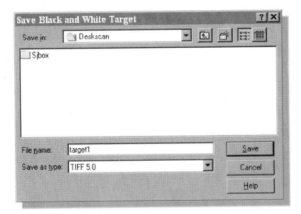

7. To save the color calibration target, click the arrow to the right of `Save as type:` Click on one of the file types (use the same file type you will be using for your scanned images). Type a name for the color calibration file in the `File name:` box. Click on **Save**. This process creates two calibration files; one for black-and-white and one for color. You must import both into your software application and scan them to calibrate for color images.

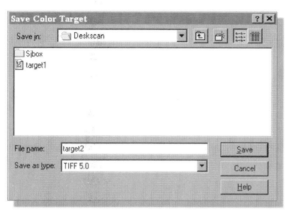

8. From the software application that you will use to print your scanned images, load or import (some applications use the term *load* and some use *import*) the calibration target files into separate pages.

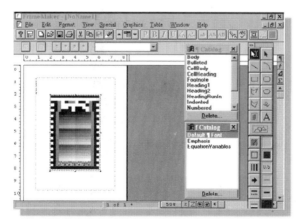

Some word processing and desktop publishing programs use frames when importing graphics (Corel Ventura, Adobe FrameMaker, QuarkXpress, etc.). For the calibration process to work, make the frames for the calibration targets 4 inches wide by 6 inches high. If the software application you are using to print the calibration targets puts registration marks, crop marks, color calibration marks, or any other type of printer markup on the page, turn these off before printing the targets.

9. Place the calibration targets in the exact center (horizontal and vertical) of the pages (see the example on the previous page).

10. Print both of the calibration pages using the same printer you will use to print your scanned images.

New printer toner cartridges print darker than ones that have been used a bit, so do not use a new printer toner cartridge when printing your print path calibration targets. If you have no choice but to use a new cartridge, print 50-100 pages before printing the target. This will stabilize the print cartridge and produce normal print levels.

11. Repeat Steps 1 — 3.

12. Click on **Scan...**

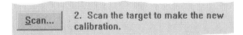

13. When both calibration target pages have printed, place the grayscale target on the scanner next to the document set mark. Align it with the top and right side of the scanner glass. Carefully close the scanner lid and click on **OK**.

14. Type a name for the calibration path (Suggestion: Use the name of your software application; i.e., `FrameMaker`).

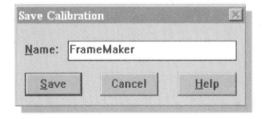

15. Click on **Save**.

16. Click on **Done**. The new calibration will now be available for use any time you scan an image that will be used with this particular software application to print to this particular printer.

> **Done** | 3. Your new calibration will now appear in the "Calibration" combo box.

Using the HP DeskScan II Controls and Tools to Get the Best Images from Your Scanner

*T*he HP DeskScan II software that came with your HP color scanner includes a number of controls and tools for correcting and enhancing your scanned images. While these controls are limited compared to an image editing program such as Adobe Photoshop, they provide the essential tools and controls you need to get a good scan. Also, it is preferable to make most corrections or enhancements prior to scanning the image to a file. This is because once an image has been scanned, editing changes the actual pixels, whereas corrections or enhancements made in DeskScan are made before the pixels are saved to a file.

Following is an illustration of the DeskScan II software (this is the Windows 95 version) that accompanied your HP ScanJet color scanner.

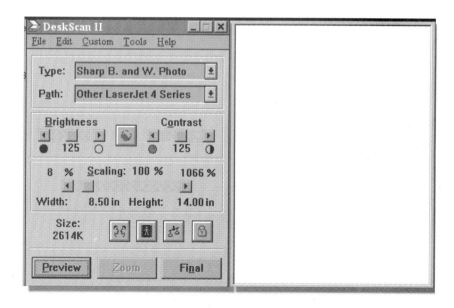

Following is an illustration of the DeskScan II software showing the major tools and controls. All of these controls are accessible from the Tools menu.

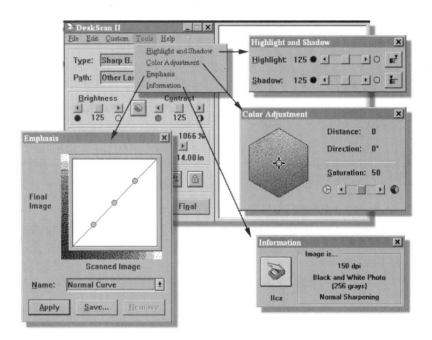

Note: In normal use, only one of the tools can be used at a time except for the Information tool (it can stay open all the time). All four are shown here at once for the purpose of illustration. The tools can be dragged and placed anywhere on the computer screen.

How to Use the Sizing and Scaling Tools

To Use Uniform Scaling

If two scaling bars are visible, *Non-Uniform Scaling* is active. If one scaling bar is visible, *Uniform Scaling* is active.

1. If two scaling bars are visible, click on the **Scale** button to switch from non-uniform to uniform scaling.

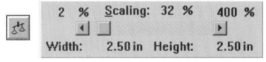

2. To simultaneously change the width and height of an image, click on the slider bar and while holding down the mouse, drag the slider bar to the right to make the image larger. Click and drag it to the left to make the image smaller.

To Use Non-Uniform Scaling

1. If one scaling bar is visible, click on the **Scale** button to switch from uniform to non-uniform scaling.

2. Click and drag the **Width** slider to change the width of the image independently of the height.

3. Click and drag the **Height** slider to change the height of the image independently of the width.

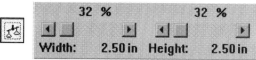

Uniform and Non-Uniform Scaling Examples

The following examples show uniform and non-uniform scaling applied to the same image.

Scanned with Non-Uniform scaling. Size: 2.5 inches width x 2.02 inches height.

Scanned with Uniform scaling. Size: 2.5 inches width x 2.5 inches height.

Scanned with Non-Uniform scaling. Size: 2.02 inches width x 2.5 inches height.

Using the Highlight and Shadow Tool to Adjust Light and Dark Areas of a Scanned Image

When shooting photographs with a camera, it is not possible to expose the dark areas (called shadows by photographers) and the light areas (called highlights) separately. The camera can only make one exposure at a time. Most cameras equipped with built-in light meters average the exposure between the shadow areas and the highlight areas. Some sophisticated cameras have spot meters which allow you to point the meter at only the shadow or highlight areas. In either case, the camera cannot expose these areas separately. Sometimes, the result is a photograph that has shadows that are too dark or highlights that are too light. In both cases, there may be detail missing from these areas that you would like to show. In a darkroom, the highlight areas can be darkened with a process called *burning in* in which the darkroom technician exposes the highlight areas longer than the rest of the photo. Shadow areas of a photo can be lightened with a technique called *dodging* in which the technician exposes the shadow areas less than the rest of the photograph. As you might imagine, these techniques require a level of skill and much practice. One-hour photo labs and most commercial photo finishing operations do not offer such services; you must use a custom photo lab and you will pay more for this service.

DeskScan II includes a Highlight and Shadow tool that you can use to separately lighten or darken shadows or highlight areas of your scanned images.

Photo scanned automatically with no use of the Highlight and Shadow tool.

Same photo scanned using the Shadow tool to lighten the shadows. Note the greater detail in the boats on the right.

How to Use the Highlight and Shadow Tool

4. Click on **Tools** on the DeskScan II menu bar, and then click on **Highlight and Shadow.**

5. DeskScan's tool windows may be moved using the mouse like any other window and placed anywhere on your screen.

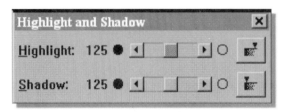

To Lighten or Darken the Highlight Areas:

1. To lighten or darken the highlight areas, click on the **Highlight** button.

2. To select the highlight point, place the special crosshairs cursor in the highlight (lightest) area of the preview image and click the mouse.

3. Place the mouse cursor on the **Highlight** slider bar. Hold down the mouse and drag the slider to the right to lighten the highlights. Drag it to the left to darken the highlights.

To Lighten or Darken the Shadow Areas:

1. To lighten or darken the shadow areas, click on the **Shadow** button.

2. To select the shadow point, place the special crosshairs cursor in the shadow (darkest) area of the preview image and click the mouse.

3. Place the mouse cursor on the **Shadow** slider bar. Hold down the mouse and drag the slider to the left to darken the shadows. Drag it to the right to lighten the shadows.

Using the Color Adjustment Tool

Why Photos Have Bad Color

Photographs can have bad or incorrect color for a number of reasons:

- **The wrong type of film**
  For example, if you shoot indoors using incandescent light with daylight film, your photos will be too red.

- **Lighting conditions**
  The color of light changes throughout the day. Photographs taken early in the morning or late in the evening will be too red.

- **Poor photo processing or printing**
  Not all photo labs or photo processing services produce good quality. If the equipment is not working properly or the operator makes a mistake, you can get prints with poor color.

How to Use the Color Adjustment Tool

1. Click on **Tools** on the DeskScan II menu bar, and then click on **Color Adjustment**.

2. The Color Adjustment tool's window may moved anywhere on your screen with your mouse.

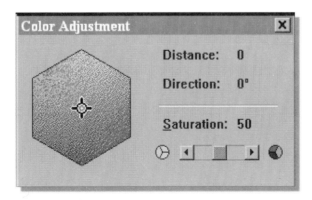

How to Change Hue with the Color Adjustment Tool

The general rule for correcting color is that you reduce the amount of one color and you add its opposite color with the Color Adjustment tool. For example, the photo shown on the bottom of the page has too much red. To remove the red, we must add its opposite color, which is cyan.

1. Place the cursor on the Color Adjustment tool's target.

2. Click and hold the mouse button. Drag the target to the desired location on the hexagon (in this case toward, cyan and away from red) and release the mouse button.

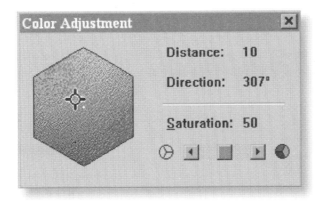

A color photo that is too red because of being shot early in the morning. To see this image in color, refer to Figure 27 in the Color Section.

The excessive red has been corrected with the Color Adjustment tool by dragging the target away from red and toward cyan. To see this image in color, refer to Figure 28 in the Color Section.

Color Adjustment Tool Examples

The following examples illustrate the results of using the Color Adjustment tool to adjust the hue. The scanned photograph in the center has no color adjustments applied. Each of the other photographs has the maximum amount of color adjustment applied. To see these examples in color, refer to Figure 29 in the Color Section.

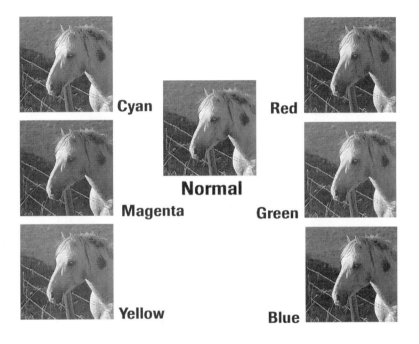

Cyan   Red

Normal

Magenta   Green

Yellow   Blue

Using the Emphasis Tool to Adjust the Contrast of a Scanned Image

The Emphasis tool is used to darken or lighten shadows, highlights, or midtones.

How to Use the Emphasis Tool

1. Click on **Tools** on the DeskScan II menu bar, and then click on **Emphasis.**

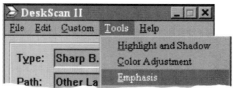

2. The Emphasis tool may moved anywhere on your screen.

3. Click on the down arrow at the right side of the Name: list box.

4. Click on one of the choices: **Normal Curve, Lighten Midtones, Darken Midtones,** or **Enhance Shadows.** Refer to the next two pages for examples of each emphasis curve.

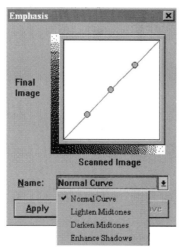

5. Click on the **Apply** button.

*For the adjustments to take effect, you must have the Emphasis tool open and visible. If you close the Emphasis tool, the Normal Curve is applied to the image. If you close the Emphasis tool without clicking **Apply**, all of the changes will be lost. This would be equivalent to clicking on a **Cancel** button.*

Emphasis Tool Examples

Following are examples of each of the built-in Emphasis tool adjustments.

Scanned using the Normal curve.

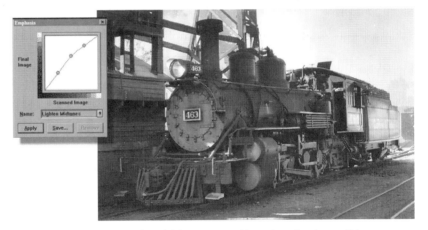

Scanned using the Lighten Midtones curve. Note that the shape of the curve is changed. The top point adjusts the highlights; the middle point adjusts the mid-tones; and the bottom point adjusts the shadows. The middle of the curve is higher than the Normal curve. The middle point has been raised, which lightens the middle tones of the image.

Scanned using the Darken Midtones curve. Note that the curve here is also different from the Normal curve. The middle of the curve is lower than normal, which darkens the middle tones.

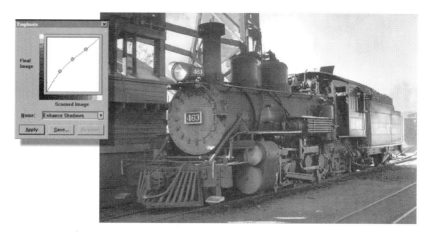

Scanned using the Enhance Shadows curve. In this case, both the shadows and mid-tone points have been moved higher, which lightens both of them. Note how much more detail you can see in the darker areas of the image.

Producing a Custom Emphasis Curve

One of the four emphasis curves that are supplied with DeskScan II will usually give you the results you want. With some images however, the supplied curves may not provide enough darkening or lightening to suit your needs or tastes. You can temporarily change the effect, or if you have a number of images that require the same changes, you can produce a custom curve and give the curve your own name.

1. Open the Emphasis tool per the instructions provided on Page 86.

2. Select the curve that is closest to the effect you want.

3. Place the cursor on one of the the points. Hold down the mouse and drag the point. Keep the following in mind:
    - The top point adjusts the highlights.
    - The middle point adjusts the mid-tones.
    - The bottom point adjusts the shadows.

4. Move a point up to lighten and down to darken. Note that the title in the name box changes to `Custom`.

5. When you have adjusted the points to your satisfaction, click **Save**...

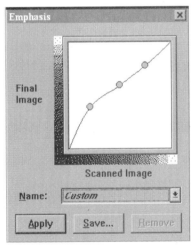

6. Type a name in the space provided and click **Save**....

7. If you wish to delete your custom curve after you no longer need it, select the custom curve's name, then click on **Remove**.

Using the Information Tool

The Information tool does what its name implies: it provides information. It provides the following information on the current image, as well as the current status of your HP ScanJet scanner:

- Model of scanner you are using
- Scanning resolution of the current image
- Current image type
- Amount of sharpening applied
- Whether you have an Automatic Document Feeder (ADF) or Transparency Adapter attached

The information that is shown will depend on the current print path and/or image type that you have chosen.

How to Use the Information Tool

1. Click on **Tools** on the DeskScan II menu bar, and then click on **Information.**

2. The Information tool may moved anywhere on your screen. Place the mouse on the title bar. Click and hold down the mouse button while dragging the tool to place it where you want it, and then release the mouse button.

3. To see more information about your HP ScanJet color scanner, click on the icon of the scanner.

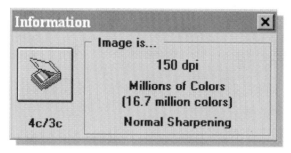

To Close the Information Tool

1. If you are using Windows 3.1 click on the **System Menus**. If you are using an Apple Macintosh, click on the **Close** box in the upper left corner. Click on **Close.**

2. If you are using Windows 95, click on the **X** in the upper right corner.

Changing the Image Type

When DeskScan II performs a preview scan, it attempts to automatically determine the image type. Most of the time, it chooses correctly and you do not need to do anything with this control. If the original is unusual in some way, such as a color photograph with very few colors, DeskScan may choose the wrong image type. You may also wish to change the setting to create a special effect.

To Change the Image Type

1. Click the down arrow on the right side of the Type: list box.

2. Click on the image type you wish to use.

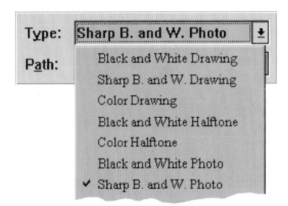

Changing the Print Path

Your HP ScanJet color scanner should have a calibrated print path for the particular printer you will be using to print your scanned images. The print path automatically determines the optimum scanning resolution to produce the best results for that particular printer. The DeskScan software includes print paths for a number of popular printers. You can use one of these when you first use your HP ScanJet scanner. As soon as possible, you should produce a custom print path for your particular printer and application software.

See Page 70 for instructions on how to create a custom print path.

To Change the Print Path

1. Click the down arrow on the right side of the Path: list box.

2. Click on the printer you wish to use.

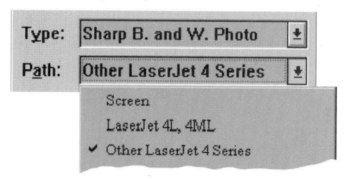

How to Enhance Fuzzy or Out-of-Focus Photographs

According to photographic industry studies, the greatest cause of dissatisfaction with personal photography is unsharp or fuzzy pictures. Fuzzy pictures are primarily caused by camera shake…that is, not holding the camera steady or using a shutter speed that is too slow. More fuzzy pictures are caused by camera shake than by poor focus. Automatic focus cameras make it much easier to focus and have reduced the number of out-of-focus pictures.

You are probably asking about now, "I have heard that scanners have a sharpening feature. Can't my HP ScanJet color scanner fix all of my fuzzy photographs?" The answer is: maybe yes, maybe no. The DeskScan II software does include a sharpening capability that can, in some cases, produce remarkable results. It can enhance a picture that is slightly fuzzy, but it cannot perform miracles!

The example on the next page shows what is possible. The original picture of a train wreck is a bit fuzzy. It was shot in poor lighting conditions, using a slow shutter speed with no tripod (sometimes we photographers are not as prepared as we should be).

I first scanned the photograph with no sharpening (HP DeskScan's defaults include sharpening, so I turned it off). Next, I scanned the same photograph with the maximum sharpening available. In this case, the photograph was made usable, but not as good as if the photograph had been sharp to begin with. I think it is safe to say that though the results may not always be perfect, in many cases using sharpening to enhance a fuzzy photo is preferable to no photograph at all.

Scanned with no sharpening.   *Scanned with Extra-Heavy sharpening.*

The sharpening process works by increasing the contrast of adjacent pixels along the edges in an image. The sharpening effect will be more apparent in photographs with small details or lettering.

You have five choices of sharpening with DeskScan II:

- None
- Light
- Normal (the DeskScan II default)
- Heavy
- Extra-Heavy

Sharpening is part of the image type selection in the custom controls of DeskScan II. See Page 91 for an explanation of how to select or customize image types. The HP DeskScan II image type defaults are set with the preferences menu. The default for drawings, black-and-white photos, color photos, and millions of colors is Normal sharpening.

Sharp Words about Sharpening

There are several things to keep in mind when using sharpening on your photographs:

- Sharpening increases the contrast of the entire image, so you may wish to compensate by lowering the contrast with DeskScan II before making the final scan.

- As sharpening increases image contrast, defects such as scratches, dust or lint spots, etc. that were present in the original photograph or were introduced during scanning (perhaps you didn't clean the scanner glass) will be emphasized. These defects may not have been apparent in an unsharpened scan of the photograph. These defects also may not have been noticeable on a 300 dpi printer, but may be apparent on a 600 dpi printer or a high-resolution imagesetter.

■ Heavy or Extra-Heavy sharpening of a color image may create an undesirable effect called a *sharpening artifact*, especially in light areas such as the sky or clouds.

■ Heavy or Extra-Heavy sharpening may cause your image to appear grainy, and if the photograph was grainy to begin with, the effect will be exaggerated.

Sharpening with an Image Editor

You may be asking at this point, "What if I want to sharpen an image that has already been scanned with no sharpening or not enough sharpening. Can I use my image editor to sharpen an already scanned image?"

You should, if possible, make as many adjustments to your images before you scan. Anything done to an image after it has been scanned results in some loss of data and perhaps detail. Having said that, it

The Adobe Photoshop Unsharp Mask filter.

is possible to use the sharpening controls in your image editor. Most image editors have a control called an unsharp mask or unsharp control. Sounds like the last thing you would want to use, but it does not do what its name implies. The term *unsharp mask* is a photography term and darkroom process. I don't want to bore you with the technical details of how this works; instead I will limit the discussion and simply say that the unsharp tool in most image editors works better than the sharpening filters and you should always use it when sharpening an image with your image editor. The unsharp filter also gives you more control over how much sharpening will be applied.

Scanned with no sharpening.

Sharpened with Photoshop's Unsharp Mask filter.

How to Sharpen Line Art

Line art or drawings can be improved with sharpening. This may seem illogical to some of you: How can a drawing or line art be out-of-focus or have camera shake? Well, it can't! However, since the sharpening software increases the contrast between the boundaries of light and dark pixels, it can also work on 1-bit line art. Drawings or line art that have fine detail or closely spaced lines will look better if sharpening is used. If you are going to use the scanned image for tracing, you will want the maximum amount of detail for the tracing program. The default for scanning a drawing with DeskScan II is Normal sharpening and that should be enough for most images. If you are scanning an original with very minute detailed lines, you may want to try Heavy or Extra-Heavy sharpening.

Scanned at 600 ppi with no sharpening.
®Dover Publications 1988

Scanned at 600 ppi with Extra-Heavy sharpening. Note the greater detail in the balloon's cables.

Using Custom Controls

DeskScan II includes four custom controls that let you change DeskScan's defaults and make your own custom options. DeskScan includes the capability to automatically determine the image type and select the image area. You may wish to change the image type either for special effects or because DeskScan did not choose the correct type.

Selecting or Creating a Custom Image Type

In Chapter 2, we learned about image types and how to choose an image type that best reproduces your original. Your HP ScanJet color scanner comes with a number of image type selections that will probably suit most of your needs. The HP DeskScan II software will attempt to automatically select an image type. Most of the time it gets it right and you will probably be satisfied with the automatic selection. Occasionally, you may want to use a different choice than the one DeskScan selects for you. For example, DeskScan II may select Sharp Millions of Colors. This would be a good choice for printing a color image, but suppose you want to scan an image for multimedia or the World Wide Web on the Internet. Sharp Millions of Colors may not be a good choice for multimedia or any kind of image that is to be displayed on the computer screen. What you probably need is Color Photo, which would give you 256 colors instead of millions. This will make

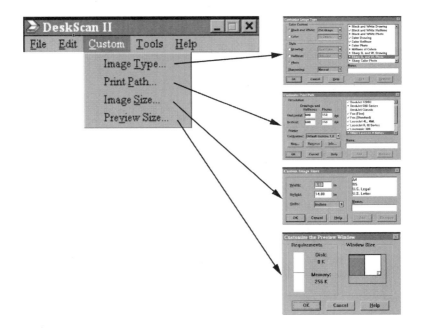

a smaller file and you sometimes don't need millions of colors for multi-media or the Web. In this case, you will want to change the image type.

To Select an Image Type

1. Click on **Custom** in the DeskScan II menu.

2. Click on **Image Type**.

3. Click on one of the image types displayed at the right. Use the scroll bar if necessary.

4. Click **OK**.

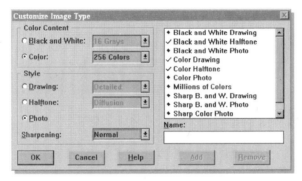

To Create a New Image Type

You may find that sometimes the standard image types that are included with DeskScan II do not suit your needs. For example, Normal sharpening is used in all of the DeskScan II standard selections. If you have a lot of images that require Heavy or Extra-Heavy sharpening, you may wish to create a custom image type that includes Heavy or Extra-Heavy sharpening. I would recommend that when creating a new image type, start with one of the included ones, make your changes, and save it as a new type.

1. Click on **Custom** in the DeskScan II menu.

2. Click on **Image Type**.

3. Click on one of the image types displayed at the right that is the closest match for what you want. Use the scroll bar if necessary.

4. Make any changes you need in the `Content` and `Style` boxes.

5. Type a name for your new image type in the `Name:` box (make the name descriptive...I named mine `Heavy Sharp Millions of Colors`.

6. Click on **OK**. Your new custom image type can be used each time you scan. It will appear in DeskScan's Type menu.

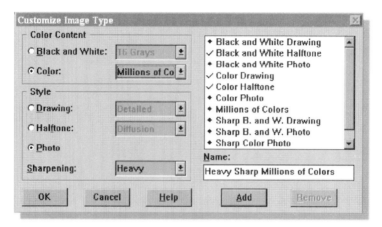

Creating or Selecting a Custom Print Path

In the beginning of this chapter, I outlined the print path process and detailed the importance of this to image quality. The print path determines the resolution of your scanned images (you can manually override the settings) and the gamma (contrast) that will be used. Your HP ScanJet's DeskScan II software includes print paths for most HP desktop printers, as well as for fax and for a high-resolution imagesetter. You can create a new print path for your own particular printer, if it is not already on the list, by following the procedures outlined on Page 70.

To Select a Print Path

1. Click on **Custom** in the DeskScan II menu.

2. Click on **Print Path** in the **Custom** menu.

3. Click on one of the printers listed (use the scroll bar if necessary to find your printer).

4. Click on **OK**.

To Create a Custom Print Path

The process of creating a custom print path is described on Page 70.

Creating or Selecting a Custom Image Size

If you regularly need to have exact image size, you can use the Custom Image Sizes dialog box to create custom, named image sizes that produce exact selection areas in the preview window. This saves time working with the scaling control.

To Select an Image Size

1. Click on **Custom** in the DeskScan II menu.

2. Click on **Image Size**.

3. Click on one of the sizes shown (A4, B5, U.S. Legal, U.S. Letter).

4. Click on **OK**.

To Create a New Image Size

1. Click on **Custom** in the DeskScan II menu.

2. Click on **Image Size**.

3. Type the width and height for your new custom image size.

4. In the Name: box, type a descriptive name for your new custom image size (I used the name square in this case).

5. Click on **Add**.

6. Click **OK**. Your new custom size can now be used to save time setting the image size each time you scan.

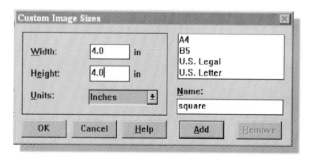

Creating a Custom Size Preview Window

The area at the right side of the DeskScan II interface is called the *Preview Area*. It is where the scanned image is displayed. You can make this Preview Area larger or smaller to suit your needs and tastes.

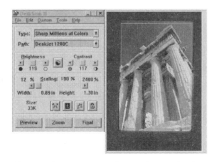

Preview Area set to minimum.

Preview Area increased to enlarge the detail in the scanned image.

1. Click on **Custom** in the DeskScan II menu.

2. Click on **Preview Size.**

3. Click on the small box (called the grow box) in the lower right corner of the left, white rectangle in the Window Size area. Hold down the mouse and drag. Drag down and right to increase the size of the preview window. Drag up and left to decrease the size.

4. Click **OK**. The new size will not take effect until you perform a new preview scan.

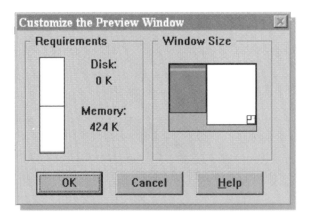

How to Select the Appropriate Resolution

*R*esolution is probably the most misunderstood part of scanning and is the most confusing aspect for new scanner users and even some users who have been scanning for years. In speaking to DTP and graphics user groups, the number one question always is: What resolution should I use? Should I scan at the maximum resolution of the scanner? I have a 600 dpi printer, shouldn't I always scan at 600 ppi?

Resolution is not an easy concept to grasp. I will first explain some concepts and terms that you need to know if you are going to understand what happens when you scan and print an image. Second, I will give you some guidelines and tips that will help you to select the resolution that will give you optimum printed output and yet not take up your entire hard disk.

There are actually four resolutions that we must discuss when trying to understand scanning resolution:

- **Scanning Resolution**
  This is the resolution of your scanned data. It is often expressed as *dots-per-inch* or *pixels-per-inch*. In this book, I will use *pixels-per-inch* or *ppi* when describing scanned images to differentiate from printed images, for which I will use dots-per-inch (dpi). Just remember that dots are round and pixels are square. Scanners do not scan in round dots, but in square pixels.

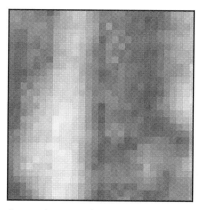

Scanned image enlarged to show the square pixels.

Scan of a printed page enlarged to show the printer dots.

■ **Monitor Resolution**

This is sometimes referred to as screen resolution, but I will use the term "monitor" to avoid confusion with line screen resolution when talking about printers. Computer monitors have resolution. Your word processor, image editor, and scanned images are displayed on a grid consisting of rows of small black-and-white or colored squares called picture elements or pixels. Often you will see monitor resolution described with dots-per-inch. Technically, this is not correct as the monitors do not display dots, but pixels. Most computer monitor screens have a resolution of from 70 to 100 pixels-per-inch.

■ **Printer Resolution**

It is correct to refer to printer resolution as dots-per-inch as printers print with dots (they may be oddly-shaped dots). Desktop printers use dots of toner or dots of ink to print text and line art; they group the dots into halftone patterns to create the illusion of continuous tone grayscale or color photographs. Desktop printers typically have resolutions ranging from 72 to 600 dots-per-inch and high resolution imagesetters have resolutions ranging from 1250 to over 5000 dots-per-inch.

■ **Line Screen Resolution**

This is also known as line screen frequency. Before computer publishing and imaging, photographs were included in books and magazines by copying them with special cameras using glass or plastic halftone or line screens. These screens were etched with a pattern of tiny clear dots. When the original photographs were copied through these screens onto special film, the resulting image consisted of thousands of tiny dots. These dots created the illusion of continuous shades of gray or color when you looked at a photograph in a book, magazine, or document. Dots on screens are arranged in rows. The number of these rows per inch is the line screen frequency and the number of rows determines the resolution of the printed image. Computer publishing and imaging use software and hardware to produce the halftoning effect created by the line screen.

So, What Is the Appropriate Resolution?

Determining the optimum resolution to use when scanning an image depends on several variables:

■ What image type is the original?

- Will the image be halftoned?
- What will be the final output (desktop printer, commercial printing press, online such as the World Wide Web, etc.)?
- Will the original be enlarged or reduced (scaled) during scanning?

In almost all cases it is not necessary or even advisable to scan at the highest possible resolution, the standard resolution of the scanner, or even the resolution of the printer. This is difficult for many to understand. Why would I not want to scan at the maximum resolution possible? Wouldn't that give me the best possible quality? With the exception of line art (drawings), you do not need to use the maximum resolution because of the way that images are halftoned during printing. Scanning at the highest resolution or at the resolution of the printer does not give you higher quality, it simply makes the file larger than is necessary and increases your printing time. If your desktop printer has limited memory (RAM), it might not be able to print your scanned image. Lowering the resolution of the scanned image to the optimum may let you print in that case. If you regularly send documents with scanned images to a high-resolution service bureau or commercial printer, scanning images at resolutions that are higher than necessary can cost you significantly.

The Appropriate Resolution Is in the Print Path

Because the appropriate resolution in most cases is directly related to the printer being used, the HP DeskScan II software incorporates resolution into the print path calibration process. Your HP ScanJet color scanner is calibrated to the printer you will be using for proofing or for final output. Following is an example of this:

You are using an HP DeskJet desktop color printer to print your scanned images. This printer has a resolution of 300 dpi and a line screen frequency of 45 lines-per-inch with a screen angle of 45 degrees. The guidelines for scanning resolution tell you that you should use a scanning resolution that is 1- ½ times that of the line screen. 1- ½ times 45 (the screen angle of the DeskJet Printer)is 67.5. This means you should scan images that will be printed on that printer at 67.5 pixels-per-inch. You should always use even numbers for resolution, so round 67.5 to 70 or 75 pixels-per-inch.

What If I Want to Choose my Own Resolution?

The best way to get the optimum resolution for your scanned images is to use one of the print paths provided with the HP DeskScan II software or to create a custom print path. By using a print path, you do not have to manually enter a resolution number each time you scan. Also, calculating the optimum resolution can be done one time and you don't have to worry about making a mistake.

There is one significant case where you will want to manually enter a resolution number. If you are enlarging or reducing during the scanning process, you will want to increase or decrease the resolution. The DeskScan II print path calibration process is based on no scaling (scanning at 100%). There is no automatic way for DeskScan II to account for scaling.

Refer to Pages 109 - 110 for charts that will help you select the appropriate resolution.

How to Manually Enter a Custom Scan Resolution

1. Click on **Custom** in the DeskScan II menu, and then click on **Print Path.**

2. Click on the printer you will be using for your final output
   (this will provide the proper starting point for selecting a custom resolution).

3. Type in new resolution numbers in the appropriate dialog boxes under `Photos` or `Drawings and Halftones`. DeskScan II supports scanning at different resolutions for horizontal and vertical, so you must enter resolution numbers in both the Horizontal and Vertical fields.

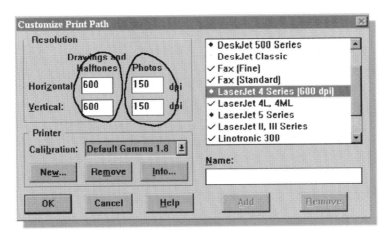

4. Click **OK.**

What Resolution to Use for Drawings or Halftones

When you save scanned images as drawings or halftones, there is no halftoning performed on these images when they are printed. Drawings or images that are being saved as halftones should be scanned at the resolution of the printer that will be used for the final output. If you will be using a 600 dpi laser printer for your final output, you should scan at 600 ppi. Scanning at the resolution of the printer helps to reduce or eliminate jaggies. It also provides the best starting point for converting an image to a vector graphic with a tracing program such as Adobe Streamline or Corel TRACE.

Refer to Chapter 8 for a description of the tracing process.

What Resolution to Use for Black-and-White or Color Photos

Selecting the appropriate resolution for black-and-white or color photographs is more complex than selecting the resolution for drawings. Black-and-white and color photographs must be halftoned before they can be printed on a desktop printer or a commercial printing press. In Chapter 3, I described the halftoning process. To refresh your memory, halftoning is the process in which an original image is converted to various sized dots. The impression of continuous tone is created by grouping the dots. Large dots grouped close together create the impression of black or saturated areas. Smaller dots grouped further apart create the visual impression of gray or medium-colored areas. Even smaller dots grouped even further apart create the visual impression of light gray, white, or very light-colored areas. The grouping of these dots is based on the screen frequency (lines-per-inch), the angle of the halftone screen, and the shape of the dots. We will discuss the screen angle in more detail later in the chapter as this is very important when printing color images with a commercial printing press.

In traditional printing, an original image is copied onto photographic film to create a transparent positive copy. Light is passed through the positive copy and through the halftone screen onto another sheet of photographic film. The continuous toned images are then converted to a pattern of round dots.

High-resolution imagesetters and most desktop printers cannot produce dots of different sizes. All the dots are the same size. To print grayscale or color images, these printers group same-size dots to produce the impression of larger dots. These digital dots are called *halftone cells*. The way these same-size dots are grouped is determined by the halftone screen frequency. With traditional glass halftone screens, the number of lines in the grid determines the screen frequency. A typical screen has 133 lines-per-inch. In electronic publishing, the halftone screening process is accomplished electronically. Electronic halftoning can be done by the scanner, by the printer, by the software application, or by software called a *printer driver*. In computer halftoning, the square pixels of the scanned image are converted to a pattern of round dots.

The reason you do not have to scan at the maximum resolution of the scanner or the resolution of the printer is the halftoning process. The square pixels of the scanned image are converted to round halftone dots. In effect, you are converting one grid (pixels) to another grid (halftone dots).

If you can think of the halftoning process as water passing through a filter it might be easier to understand. A water filter has tiny holes or openings that form a grid (a halftone screen filters light like a water filter filters water). The grid determines how much and how fast the water can pass through the filter. If you attempt to pour more water through the filter than it can accommodate, the water will spill over the edges and will not pass through. This is what happens when you scan an image at a higher resolution than necessary. There is an optimum resolution for the halftone screen frequency of the printer you are using. If you scan at a resolution that is higher than this optimum resolution, the data will be discarded by the halftone screening process.

So now that we have determined that the controlling factor in determining scanning resolution of black-and-white or color photographs is screen frequency, how do we use that to select the appropriate scanning resolution. Years of experience in printing continuous tone images has taught professionals what works and what does not. The general rule that printing professionals have developed is that the optimum resolution is 1-½ times the screen frequency of the printer used for final output. This is called the *halftone ratio*. Some professionals use a halftone ratio of 1-¼ or 2.

I have included three charts to help you select the appropriate resolution based on the halftone line screen used, the size of the image, and the halftone ratio. I have included charts for halftone ratios of 1.25 (1-¼), 1.50 (1-½), and 2.0. To use the charts, find the line screen you will be using along the left edge. If you don't know (ask your service bureau or refer to the next paragraph for instructions on how to determine line screen on a desktop printer). Next, find the size percentage along the bottom of the chart (if you are not scaling the image, this will be 100%). Where the two intersect, the number will be the resolution you should use to scan your images for that printer.

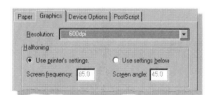

Line Screen

133 lpi	49	99	149	199	249
150 lpi	56	112	168	225	281
175 lpi	65	131	196	262	328
200 lpi	75	150	225	300	375
Size	25%	50%	75%	100%	125%

Size

Resolution in PPI

If you use a desktop printer for proofing and print your final output using a high-resolution imagesetter, use the screen frequency of the imagesetter and not the desktop printer. If your printer uses a halftone screen with a frequency of 85 lines-per-inch (that is what a 600 dpi Postscript laser printer uses), your optimum scanning resolution would be 1-½ times 85, which equals 127.5. You would round that off to 130 pixels per inch.

You can determine the screen frequency used by your printer by referring to your printer's documentation or by looking at the properties of your printer's software. With many printers, you can click on the print command in your application, which brings up the printing dialog for your printer. Click on **Setup,** then click on **Graphics** and you will see a dialog box similar to the one shown below (for the HP LaserJet 4MP).

The dialog shows the screen frequency and screen angle currently used by the printer (the 4MP uses a screen frequency of 85 when printing with Postscript). You have the option of using the printer's settings or entering your own. I don't recommend entering your own unless you have a lot of experience with printing.

The screen frequency is related to the resolution of the printer. In general, 300 dpi printers have a default screen frequency of 60 lines-per-inch (see illustration below of the printer properties dialog for the HP DeskJet 1200C/PS). 600 dpi printers normally have a screen frequency of 85 lines-per-inch. High-resolution imagesetters will have screen frequencies from 95 to over 150. If your scanned images are to be printed on a high-resolution imagesetter you will have to ask the service bureau or commercial printer what screen frequency to use.

If your images will be printed on a high-resolution imagesetter and then a commercial printing press, you should calibrate your scanner for the printing press. See Page 215 for instructions on how to calibrate your scanner for a commercial printing press.

Chart for Minimum Scanning Resolution [1.25 Halftone Ratio]

Line Screen	25%	50%	75%	100%	125%	150%	175%	200%	250%	300%	350%	400%	450%	500%	1000%
50 lpi	16	32	47	63	78	94	110	125	156	187	219	250	282	313	625
60 lpi[1]	19	38	57	75	94	113	131	150	188	225	263	300	338	375	750
80 lpi[2]	25	50	75	100	125	150	175	200	250	300	350	400	450	500	1000
100 lpi	32	63	94	125	156	188	219	250	313	375	438	500	563	625	1250
120 lpi	38	75	113	150	188	225	263	300	375	450	525	600	675	750	1500
133 lpi	42	83	125	166	208	250	290	332	415	498	581	664	747	830	1660
150 lpi	47	93	140	186	233	279	325	372	465	558	651	744	837	930	1860
175 lpi	55	110	164	219	274	329	383	438	548	657	767	876	986	1095	2190
200 lpi	63	125	188	250	313	375	438	500	625	750	875	1000	1125	1250	2500
Final Size	25%	50%	75%	100%	125%	150%	175%	200%	250%	300%	350%	400%	450%	500%	1000%

The resolutions shown are the minimum necessary to print the corresponding line screen. When selecting a resolution number, round off the number to the next highest even number. For example, round off 263 ppi to 270 ppi. The formula used for calculating scanning resolution is (Halftone Ratio) X (Line Screen) X (Final Size). Final Size is determined by dividing the output size by the original size. (Thanks to Steve Toye for providing the original chart from which the others were developed.)

[1] This is the recommended line screen for a 300 dpi printer.

[2] This is the recommended line screen for a 600 dpi printer. (HP LaserJet 4 and 5 printers use an 85 lpi screen.)

Chart for Minimum Scanning Resolution [1.50 Halftone Ratio]

Line Screen	25%	50%	75%	100%	125%	150%	175%	200%	250%	300%	350%	400%	450%	500%	1000%
50 lpi	18	37	56	75	93	112	131	150	187	225	262	300	337	375	750
60 lpi[1]	22	45	67	90	112	135	157	180	225	270	315	360	405	450	900
80 lpi[2]	30	60	90	120	150	180	210	240	300	360	420	480	540	600	1200
100 lpi	37	75	112	150	187	225	262	300	375	450	525	600	675	750	1250
120 lpi	45	90	135	180	225	270	315	360	450	540	630	720	810	900	1800
133 lpi	49	99	149	199	249	299	349	399	498	598	698	798	897	997	1995
150 lpi	56	112	168	225	281	337	393	450	562	675	787	900	1012	1125	2250
175 lpi	65	131	196	262	328	393	459	525	656	787	918	1050	1181	1312	2625
200 lpi	75	150	225	300	375	450	525	600	750	900	1050	1200	1350	1500	3000
Final Size	25%	50%	75%	100%	125%	150%	175%	200%	250%	300%	350%	400%	450%	500%	1000%

The resolutions shown are the minimum necessary to print the corresponding line screen. When selecting a resolution number, round off the number to the next highest even number. For example, round off 263 ppi to 270 ppi. The formula used for calculating scanning resolution is (Halftone Ratio) X (Line Screen) X (Final Size). Final Size is determined by dividing the output size by the original size. (Thanks to Steve Toye for providing the original chart from which the others were developed.)

[1] This is the recommended line screen for a 300 dpi printer.

[2] This is the recommended line screen for a 600 dpi printer. (HP LaserJet 4 and 5 printers use an 85 lpi screen.)

Chart for Minimum Scanning Resolution [2.0 Halftone Ratio]

Line Screen	25%	50%	75%	100%	125%	150%	175%	200%	250%	300%	350%	400%	450%	500%	1000%
50 lpi	25	50	75	100	125	150	175	200	250	300	350	400	450	500	1000
60 lpi [1]	30	60	90	120	150	180	210	240	300	360	420	480	540	600	1200
80 lpi [2]	40	80	120	160	200	240	280	320	400	480	560	640	720	800	1600
100 lpi	50	100	150	200	250	300	350	400	500	600	700	800	900	1000	2000
120 lpi	60	120	180	240	300	360	420	480	600	720	840	960	1080	1200	2400
133 lpi	66	133	199	266	332	399	465	532	665	798	931	1064	1197	1330	2660
150 lpi	75	150	225	300	375	450	525	600	750	900	1050	1200	1350	1500	3000
175 lpi	87	180	262	350	437	525	612	700	900	1050	1225	1400	1575	1750	3500
200 lpi	100	200	300	400	500	600	700	800	1000	1200	1400	1600	1800	2000	4000
Final Size	25%	50%	75%	100%	125%	150%	175%	200%	250%	300%	350%	400%	450%	500%	1000%

The resolutions shown are the minimum necessary to print the corresponding line screen. When selecting a resolution number, round off the number to the next highest even number. For example, round off 263 ppi to 270 ppi. The formula used for calculating scanning resolution is (Halftone Ratio) X (Line Screen) X (Final Size). Final Size is determined by dividing the output size by the original size. (Thanks to Steve Toye for providing the original chart from which the others were developed.)

[1] This is the recommended line screen for a 300 dpi printer.

[2] This is the recommended line screen for a 600 dpi printer. (HP LaserJet printers use a 85 lpi screen.)

What Is Interpolation?

Interpolation is a technique for increasing perceived resolution. It is a software process in which new pixels are created between original pixels in a scanned image. Interpolation creates these new pixels by dividing the original or existing pixels.

The process also calculates the range of hues between adjacent pixels and creates new pixels that are an average of the two. This creates a smooth gradation between the original pixels.

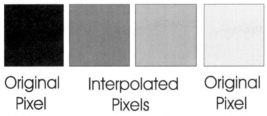

Original   Interpolated   Original
Pixel   Pixels   Pixel

It is important to remember that interpolation does not increase the actual resolution of your scanner. Interpolation is a software process that creates new pixels that are an average of existing ones. Interpolation creates greater detail in your scanned images. Interpolation works better with drawings and line art than it does with grayscale or color photographs, but it is effective for both.

Interpolation increases the perceived resolution of your HP ScanJet scanner. It does not increase the actual resolution. An HP ScanJet 4c color scanner has an actual resolution of 600 pixels-per-inch. Interpolation increases the perceived resolution to 2400 pixels-per-inch. I recommend that you use interpolation with care. It can be helpful with drawings and line art that must be enlarged or scaled after they have been scanned. It can also be useful in scanning drawings or line art that are to be traced.

Chapter 6

How to Use Scanned Images with Software Applications

Introduction

Now that you have mastered the techniques of using your HP ScanJet scanner and you have beautiful scanned images, how do you get them into the software that you use everyday to produce graphics, documents, and publications? This chapter will highlight most major application types and will illustrate how to use your scanned images with these applications. While space does not permit detailed instructions on particular software titles, the tips and techniques provided should apply to most of your software programs.

What Can You Do with Scanned Images?

Most software applications will let you import graphical images including scanned images. Even programs not typically thought of as graphical programs such as spreadsheets will now import graphic files such as scanned images. You can include scanned images of products or people in financial reports. It would be difficult to find a word processing program that did not import at least some graphical file formats such TIFF. You can now produce professional, high-quality documents that include scanned photographs or drawings with your word processing program. More examples of combining scanned images with software applications include:

- You can include scanned photographs and drawings in word processing documents.

- You can produce newsletters, magazines, and books with desktop publishing programs and include black-and-white or color photos and scanned clip art.

- You can import scanned images into drawing or illustration programs and make them a part of a drawing, or you can trace the images to make them drawings.

- You can scan a drawing or clip art and add depth with a 3D program.

- With image editors such as Adobe Photoshop and Corel PHOTO-PAINT, you can work magic on your images.

- You can scan text from documents and convert the scans to word processing files.

Word Processors

*O*nly a few years ago, word processing software was strictly for text creation and editing. Then, a few applications added the capability to create or import simple graphics such as bar charts created by spreadsheets. Today, any self-respecting text editor or word processor includes the capability to import most graphical file formats including those produced by HP ScanJet scanners.

Most word processors have become so sophisticated and feature-laden that they can compete with many desktop publishing (DTP) programs. Documents that previously could only be produced with a DTP program such as Adobe PageMaker, Corel Ventura Publisher, or QuarkXpress, can now be created with Microsoft Word or Corel WordPerfect. Most word processing programs now also have the capability to produce multiple columns, ruling lines, drop caps, etc.

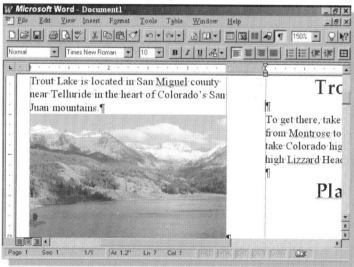

Scanned image imported into Microsoft Word for Windows. Image is centered in a column of a two-column layout.

One advantage that DTP programs offer over most word processors is control over the placement of scanned images. Some word processors only allow you to place images on the left side, right side, or center of the page. Some word processing programs place scanned images into the text flow and treat the images the same as text.

Word processing programs typically do not provide any image editing or control features such as contrast or brightness, so your scanned image should be ready for printing. Make all corrections, edits, or adjustments when you scan the image with DeskScan II or with your image editor.

If your image needs are simple, a word processing program will probably give you all the features and control that you need. Many of these programs let you resize an image (although you shouldn't do this), crop parts of the image (this is OK), or place lines around the image. If you need sophisticated image capabilities such as rotation or special text wrapping around images, you should look at the DTP programs described later in this chapter.

You can include grayscale or color scanned photographs or line art in most word processors using TWAIN or by importing previously scanned files. If your word processor does not support TWAIN, you may be able to use OLE (Object Linking and Embedding) to bring the image in from an image editor. If you can't use TWAIN or OLE, you will have to use the traditional file importing feature of your program.

The following examples illustrate how one program (Microsoft Word for Windows) imports graphics using file import or OLE. Most word processing programs import graphics using a similar procedure.

Importing a Scanned Image into MS Word with the Insert Picture Command

1. Click on **Insert**.

2. Click on **Picture**...

3. Click on the arrow at the left side of `Look in:` to select the folder or directory where the image is saved. Click on a file in the list.

4. To select a particular file type, click on the arrow at the left side of `File of type:` Click on a file type from the list. A thumbnail of the image will be displayed on the right side of the screen.

5. Click on **OK**. The image will be placed in MS Word and can be arranged on the page by using the paragraph formatting commands.

Importing a Scanned Image into MS Word with OLE

1. Start MS Word.

2. Create or load the document you wish to place the image in.

3. Click on **Insert**.

4. Click on **Object...**

5. Click on an Object Type from the list. Examples of object types include: Adobe Acrobat files, bitmap images, etc.

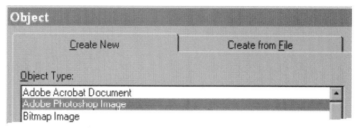

6. Click **OK**.

7. The image will be placed in MS Word and can be arranged on the page by using the paragraph formatting commands.

OLE cannot work unless the application that created the graphic (or last saved it) is installed on the same computer as the application you are importing the image into (MS Word in this case).

Desktop Publishing

*I*t was slightly more than ten years ago that Paul Brainard, founder of Aldus Corporation (now part of Adobe), developed a software program named PageMaker and coined the term *desktop publishing*. Although pundits often disagree on what is meant by desktop publishing, in this book I use the term to describe software that is more advanced than most word processing software and that gives you the capability to produce professional-level and professional-quality publications for personal or commercial publishing.

In the beginning, all desktop publishing software was designed for users who wanted high-quality, professional publishing. Programs such as Adobe PageMaker, QuarkXPress, Adobe FrameMaker, and Corel Ventura were and are primarily for users who publish documents as a major part of their activities. These programs offer features for those who produce long documents or documents that require precise control over image placement and typographic features. Originally, PageMaker and QuarkX-Press used a paste-up metaphor similar to the traditional method of pasting text, photographs, and drawings onto cardstock with wax or glue. FrameMaker and Ventura differed from PageMaker and XPress by using a tag metaphor to format text and graphics. It was said that FrameMaker and Ventura were for highly structured, long documents while PageMaker and QuarkXPress were for short documents that were free-form. In recent years, XPress and PageMaker have added tags or styles, while FrameMaker and Ventura have offered more free-form design features.

In recent years, new DTP software has been introduced that is not designed for traditional professional publishing. Products like Microsoft Publisher offer more features than most word processors, but do not include all the bells and whistles of programs like PageMaker and QuarkXPress. These programs were designed for those who occasionally publish a group or church newsletter, small business documents, etc. While this category of publishing software does not offer the full range of capabilities of the high-level programs, most of these programs incorporate the capability to include scanned images either directly with TWAIN or through file import.

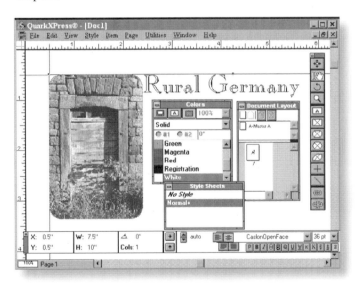

QuarkXPress is available in both Macintosh and Windows versions (version 3.3 for Windows is shown). XPress is a favorite of newspaper and magazine publishers. Many add-on programs (called XTensions) are available that extend the program's capabilities.

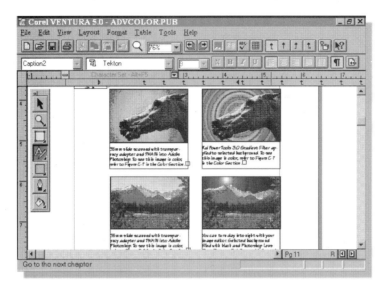

*Corel Ventura Publisher 5.0. This is the desktop publishing
program I used to produce this book. Ventura was previously available in a Macintosh version, but current versions are Windows-only. Ventura is a frame-based program,
meaning all text and graphics are imported into frames.*

*Adobe FrameMaker 5 is available in Windows, Macintosh,
and UNIX versions. It offers the capability to anchor graphics to text so that as text is added or deleted the graphics move with the text automatically.*

Drawing or Illustration Software

*C*omputer graphics programs are one of two types:

- Programs that work with or use bitmapped images. These are commonly called "image editors" or "paint programs."

- Programs that work with or use vector images or graphics. These are commonly called "drawing" or "illustration" programs.

  See Page 148 for an explanation of bitmapped and vector images.

Drawing or illustration programs normally work with lines, circles, and objects rather than bitmapped images such as scanned images. These programs typically work with vector graphic formats such as DFX (Auto-CAD format), HPGL (Hewlett-Packard Graphics Language), and Encapsulated PostScript.

The most popular drawing or illustration programs are CorelDRAW (both Mac and Windows) and Adobe Illustrator (Mac and Windows). Other highly capable drawing programs include Macromedia FreeHand (Mac and Windows), and Micrographx Designer (Windows only).

Drawing or illustration programs can sometimes import a bitmapped file so that it can be traced. Some can include bitmapped images as part of a drawing. But you can only print the bitmapped image, you cannot edit or modify the bitmapped image with the drawing program. If you want to produce a drawing that includes bitmapped images, be sure to do any image editing prior to importing the files into the drawing program.

You can convert a bitmapped image to a vector graphic by a process called tracing. The process is an electronic version of the tracing paper you probably used in school to trace photographs and drawings.

See Chapter 8 for more information on tracing.

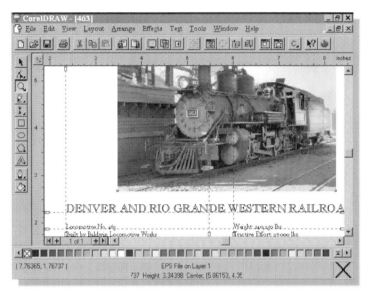

The most popular drawing program on Windows PCs is CorelDRAW and on the Mac it is Adobe Illustrator. With programs such as this, you can combine bitmapped images with drawings and text as shown here.

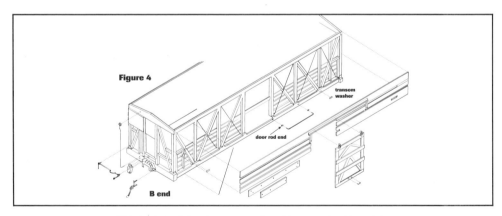

This technical drawing was produced by scanning the original drawing and tracing the scanned image with Adobe Streamline. The resulting EPS file was imported into CorelDRAW 6.0 where the text and dashed lines were added.
© San Juan Car Company.

3-D Software

*T*hree-dimensional software, commonly known as 3-D software, is a special type of illustration or drawing software. 3-D software gives you the capability to create three-dimensional graphics from two-dimensional drawings. There are a number of these programs available for both Macintosh and Windows. The capabilities include extrusion, shading, rotation, etc. You can even create multimedia animations.

To use this type of software with your HP ScanJet scanner, you must scan a drawing, trace it, and save it as a vector file format that can be imported by the 3-D program (usually EPS or DFX formats work well). Once you have imported a traced object, you can give it 3-D qualities. The following example, using Macromedia Extreme 3D, illustrates the process:

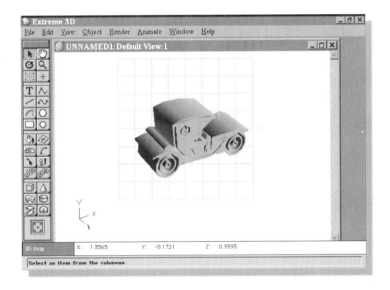

Original clip art scanned at 200 ppi.

Traced clip art extruded with Macromedia Extreme 3D software.

Image Editors

Your HP ScanJet color scanner includes a software program that is normally called an image editor. This type of software is also called paint software. When this type of software was first developed, it was rather crude and attempted to duplicate traditional oil color or water color painting. As this type of software has evolved and been given additional features, many of the programs have taken on the functionality and in some cases, the appearance of a photographic darkroom while retaining the traditional painting features.

Image editing software has become a very powerful and creative software category. With one of these programs and your HP ScanJet color scanner, you have many of the capabilities of a photographic darkroom on your desktop. You have almost unlimited options and capabilities to manipulate your scanned images. You can remove unwanted objects in scanned photographs such as a telephone pole sticking out of someone's head or a person from a group photograph (ex-wives, ex-husbands, etc.). You can correct poor color in a photograph caused by incorrect lighting or the wrong choice of film. You can combine two or more photographs to create montages. Text can be added to scanned photographs or line art to create advertisements, presentation slides, etc.

At the time this book was written, the Macintosh version of the HP ScanJet 4c included the light version of Adobe Photoshop with a special offer from Adobe to upgrade to the full version of Photoshop. The Windows version of the HP ScanJet 4c included Corel PHOTO-PAINT version 5. Both of these programs are very powerful image editing programs with many image manipulation features and color correction capabilities, and they include filters that let you create special or unusual effects. The full versions of Adobe Photoshop and Corel PHOTO-PAINT both support a feature called "plug-ins" that let you use additional filters produced by other companies for even greater options and choices.

See "Have Fun with Image Editor Filters" on Page 172.

Other highly capable (but not as popular) image editors are available. On the high end for graphic professionals you will find such programs as Macromedia xRes, etc. Recently, several new programs with limited capabilities and that feature a much shorter learning curve have been introduced. If your image editing needs are not advanced, you may wish to look at programs such as Adobe PhotoDeluxe (see next page).

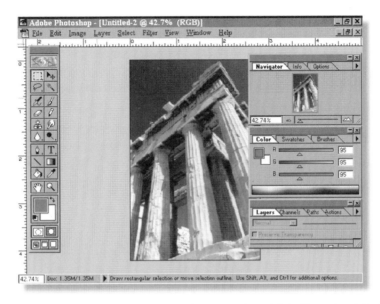

Shown above is the most popular image editor, Adobe Photoshop (this is version 4.0). Photoshop includes all the features and tools that most of us could ever possibly use to edit and manipulate scanned images.

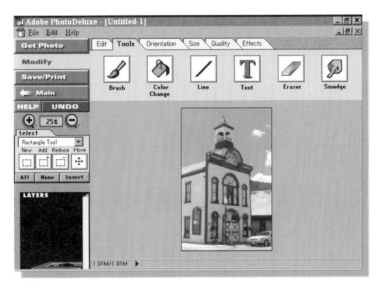

Adobe PhotoDeluxe (available for both Macintosh and Windows) is one of several new image editors for non-professionals. It emphasizes ease-of-use and provides a step-by-step user interface.

You might ask, why do I need an image editor when I can do so much with the DeskScan II software that accompanies my ScanJet scanner? The DeskScan II software is very capable indeed. You should do as much with the DeskScan II software as you can. Any time you make any changes with an image editor you are reducing data in the scanned image file.

However, there are things that DeskScan II cannot do. It does not provide all of the image manipulation and enhancement controls of a good image editor. With built-in filters and the addition of plug-in filters, you can be as creative with your scanned images as your imagination lets you.

Refer to Page 172 for an explanation of image editor filters.

35mm slide scanned into Adobe Photoshop with the transparency adapter and TWAIN. To see this image in color, refer to Figure 30 in the Color Section.

Kai Power Tools 3.0 Gradient Filter applied to selected background. To see this image in color, refer to Figure 31 in the Color Section.

35mm slide scanned into Adobe Photoshop with the transparency adapter and TWAIN. To see this image in color, refer to Figure 32 in the Color Section.

You can turn day into night with your image editor. Selected background filled with black and Photoshop Lens Flare filter applied. To see this image in color, refer to Figure 33 in the Color Section.

If you need to scan large photographs at high resolutions, you might want to take a look at Macromedia xRes2. This image editor offers the capability to load and edit large files. It uses special technology to load only part of an image file. As it only loads part of the image at one time, it can rapidly edit large files. It is available in both Macintosh and Windows versions.

Macromedia xRes 2 is a relatively new image editor. It offers the advantage of being able to load and edit large image files.

Optical Character Recognition

*O*ptical character recognition software (usually abbreviated OCR) is special software that scans typewritten or printed pages and converts the scanned text from a bitmapped image to text that can be edited with your word processor. Although this book is focused primarily on image scanning, OCR is widely used in the business world and the worlds of publishing and computer graphics. It eliminates the laborious and time-consuming task of retyping documents into your word processor.

You might ask, why not just get the text or word processing file that was used to create the document in the first place. If you can do that...fine, but you might not always have that option. Perhaps the document was not created on a computer (I know that seems hard to believe in these days of PCs and word processors, but there are still some typewriters left). Perhaps the document is old and was created before computers were even invented. I write history books and much of my research is from old newspapers and documents, many of which date from the late 1880's and early 1900's. It is much easier to scan the documents with OCR software than to retype all that text.

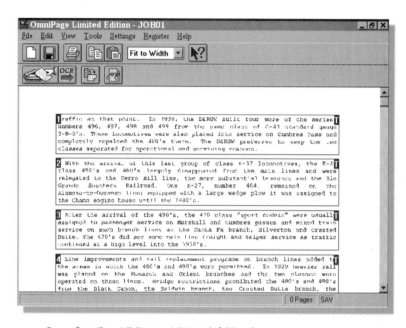

Caere OmniPage LE (Limited Edition) OCR software is included with the latest HP ScanJet scanners. You can upgrade to the full retail version for a special upgrade price.

If you plan to use the OCR capability of your HP ScanJet scanner on a regular basis, you may wish to purchase the optional document feeder attachment. All HP ScanJet scanners from the ScanJet Plus to the latest HP ScanJet 4c offer a document feeder as an optional attachment. The latest ScanJet 4c document feeder has a capacity of 50 pages and can accept documents from 5x7 inches (127mm x 178mm) to 8.5x14 inches (215mm

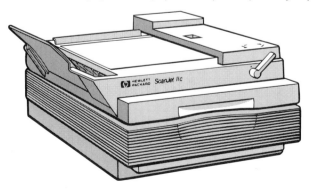

HP ScanJet IIcx with optional document feeder attached.

x 356mm). The document feeder attaches directly to the scanner, replacing the normal lid (top).

Since the introduction of the HP ScanJet IIcx in 1993, all ScanJets have included an HP patented technology called HP AccuPage. This feature combines hardware and software technology to provide the capability to recognize text as small as 5–7 points. AccuPage also provides the capability to recognize text that is on a colored or stained background (so you can recover the text on that important document that you spilled coffee on–career saving technology?). AccuPage also has the capacity to separate text from photographs or drawings and optimizes each separately.

CAD (Computer-Aided Design)

*C*omputer-Aided Design or Computer-Aided Drafting (both are referred to as CAD) programs are special types of computer illustration software. CAD software is used to design products, buildings, etc. It wasn't that long ago that CAD software was only available on high-end mainframe or mini-computer systems. Now, powerful CAD software is available on both Macintosh and Windows personal computers. Some programs, such as Autodesk AutoCAD, are for professional, technical, and very demanding users. These high-end programs are very expensive and not for someone who only occasionally produced technical illustrations. Recently, lower-cost programs have become available for those who do not perform computer-aided design or drafting as their main job. These programs, such as TurboCAD, are relatively inexpensive and easy to learn. Many of these programs are available for both Macintosh and Windows computers, but some are available on only one system.

While these programs do not normally import bitmapped images, you can use your HP ScanJet scanner and tracing software to produce files that a CAD program can import. You may have old blueprints or drawings that were produced prior to the proliferation of computers. Perhaps you have a sketch or paper drawing that you wish to use as the starting point for a computer drawing. You can scan the sketch or drawing, then use special tracing software or one of the drawing programs with tracing capabilities, to convert the bitmapped image to a vector graphic in a file format such as AutoCAD's SLD.

Refer to Chapter 8 for a description of the tracing process.

Importing Scanned Images

Most computer software includes the capability to import graphic files. Even programs that you may not normally associate with graphics, such as project management, now include graphic file import capability. The world has become more graphical and readers and users of documents now expect to see drawings, photographs, or both. The following tips and suggestions apply to most types of software programs and can be considered to be generic:

■ Do not enlarge or scale scanned images. I know all the application software lets you do this and it seems so natural. If you remember anything from this book, remember this...**scan an image at the size you plan to use it**. If the image will be 4 x 5 inches in your printed document, scan it at 4 x 5 inches.

Scanning images at the size you ultimately need does a number of good things for you. It prevents the images from becoming jagged. It saves disk space and cuts down on transmission times when you email or transfer files. If will also reduce printing time, if you have been making images larger than need be.

■ If you are bound and determined to ignore the first recommendation in this list, use whole number multiples when you enlarge or scale an image. What I mean by this is, when you enlarge, enlarge 2 times, 4 times, 8 times...not 2.3 times, 4.4 times, 8.7 times, etc. This will help to keep the image from becoming distorted and will help to keep the jaggies from getting out of hand.

■ Don't enlarge or scale scans of originals that have already been halftoned (images from magazine, books, etc.).

Never scan copyrighted or registered materials without permission. This is a crime in the U.S. and in most other countries.

■ Determine what file formats your software application will import before scanning an image. If your application requires a file format that is not supported by your HP DeskScan software you can convert a file to a different format with one of the image editors or a file conversion program such as Quarterdeck HiJaak.

Software applications import graphics using small computer programs called file filters. Applications have a file filter for each type of graphic format (TIFF, EPS, etc.). Some software applications install all of their available filters during installation and some offer you the option of choosing the ones you want. If you don't install all of them, you may not be able to import a file later. With some applications, you can run the install program and install the filters you omitted the first time. Be sure to consult the installation instructions for your particular application.

■ Crop unnecessary and unwanted white space or borders using the selection rectangle or lasso tool in the HP DeskScan II software. In a scanned image, there is no such thing as blank space. White space is recorded as part of the image and occupies disk space on your system. If you leave too much white space when scanning, you can delete it with your image editor. Even though many DTP programs provide the capability to crop or mask scanned images, they are only hiding part of the image, not making the file smaller.

■ Some DTP programs include the capability to rotate a graphic, including scanned images. Rotated images are visually interesting, so everyone likes to do them…I included several rotated images in this book. Don't rotate images in your DTP program; this will slow your computer's display and will increase printing time because the DTP program must calculate the rotation effect each time. If you want this effect, rotate the scanned image with your image editor before importing the file into the DTP program. Some DTP programs let you wrap text around images and you can do this with a scanned image that has been rotated in the image editor.

Anytime you manipulate a scanned image with an image editor, make a backup copy of the original scanned image so that if you mess it up you can always go back and start again. (I never do this as I never make mistakes. You do believe me, don't you?).

Importing Images with TWAIN

What Is TWAIN?

TWAIN is a software interface developed by Hewlett-Packard, Aldus (Adobe), Caere, Kodak, Logitech, and other companies producing scanners and software that works with scanners. TWAIN eliminates the bothersome necessity to leave the software application you are working in to scan an image. With TWAIN you can scan directly into whatever program you are using at the time: image editor, DTP program, document manager, etc. After you scanned an image into an application, you can usually save it in one of the formats that the application supports. Sometimes the application has a default format and you must use that one. Some applications support many file formats, so your options for file formats are increased when you use TWAIN.

With TWAIN, you can run your application and the HP DeskScan II software at the same time. Applications that support TWAIN have an added File menu item called "Acquire" or "Import." When you select this command, DeskScan II starts and runs on top of your application. All the features of DeskScan II are available and you use it as you normally would.

TWAIN Scanning Example

If the software application program that you wish to place your scanned images into supports TWAIN, the process is very simple and you will continue to use the HP DeskScan II software normally. The following example using Adobe Photoshop and DeskScan II illustrates how TWAIN works.

Adobe Photoshop does not use the standard interface for TWAIN, so this example is correct only for Photoshop.

1. From the application's File menu, select **Acquire**. You will normally see two items displayed: Acquire and Select Source (some applications have additional items, but most only have two).

2. Click on **Select TWAIN Source**.

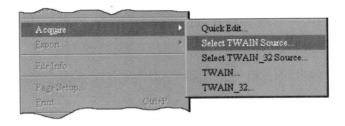

3. Click on **DeskScan II** when the choices are displayed.

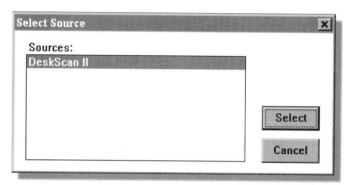

Your application is now set to use TWAIN with your HP ScanJet scanner.

4. To scan with TWAIN, select **Acquire** from the File menu.

5. Select **TWAIN**.

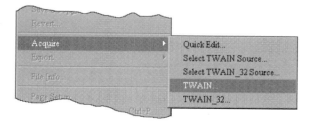

6. DeskScan II starts on top of your application and performs a preview scan. Use DeskScan II as you would if you were running it alone. (Be sure to have your original on the scanner glass.)

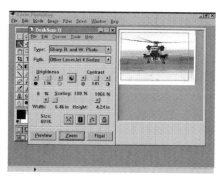

7. When you are satisfied with the DeskScan II settings, click on **Final**.

8. Your image will be scanned
   and placed in your
   application. With some
   applications, you must close
   DeskScan II to be transferred
   back to your application.
   Some applications do this
   automatically.

Not all Macintosh and Windows software applications are TWAIN-compliant. Refer to your software application user documentation to determine if it supports TWAIN and to find instructions on how to access DeskScan II directly from the application.

Chapter 7

How to Scan for the Computer Screen

Introduction

Not all scanned images are printed on paper. Increasingly, images are being scanned for display on the computer screen only. The rapid growth of multimedia which combines still images, sound, and full-motion video has created a great demand for photographs and drawings. The explosion of interest in the World Wide Web and online services such as Prodigy, America Online, and CompuServe offer a rapid and relatively inexpensive method of distributing scanned images via electronic mail, forums, and conferences. Effective Computer-Based Training (CBT) uses illustrations and photographs to convey information quickly. Tests and studies have shown that the use of graphics in training increases comprehension and retention significantly. In addition, the use of illustrations and photographs can entice reluctant readers to use the training materials.

Scanning for Multimedia

Multimedia is not easy to define. It means different things to different people. Technically, multimedia is an abbreviation of multiple media. To some folks, multimedia is the beep that your computer makes when you press the wrong key. To many, multimedia is defined as a combination of visual and verbal elements. Beyond that simple definition, multimedia can be anything from a simple graphics presentation with the addition of a recorded soundtrack of a speaker to full-frame, full-motion video with stereo sound.

This confusion over what multimedia actually means caused several manufacturers of PCs to form a group to define standards for multimedia PCs (these standards, however, applied only to MS-DOS and Windows PCs and did not include Apple Macintosh computers: Macs were already multimedia capable). This group developed a list of minimum requirements for the *MPC* (Multimedia PC) standard. This standard was upgraded recently to *MPC2* to reflect improved technology and faster PCs.

Without going into all of the gory details, the MPC standard defines a multimedia PC as a PC that includes a CD-ROM and sound card as the bare minimum to play and display multimedia productions. The experts will not agree on particular hardware and software; some will argue that you must have a 16-bit stereo sound system, while others will say that an 8-bit monaural is good enough. The MPC2 standard requires stereo, but MPC systems will run MPC2 software.

Multimedia is being used in a vast variety of creative ways to educate and entertain. Estimates are that about 8,000 CD-ROM titles are currently available and more are being produced daily. Children and adults will no longer accept computer programs that are text only. To gain and keep the attention of users of these programs they must include illustrations and photographs. Your HP ScanJet color scanner is the tool you need to incorporate drawings and black-and-white and color photographs into your multimedia programs.

Multimedia programs and presentations are created with multimedia authoring or presentation software such as Asymetrix Compel, Microsoft PowerPoint, HSC InterActive, Adobe Persuasion, Asymetrix Multimedia Toolbox, Macromedia Director, Macromedia Authorware, Autodesk Animator. These programs provide various tools for creating text and graphics and for importing illustrations, photographs, sound clips, video, etc. Many include templates consisting of backgrounds and placeholders for text and graphics. These templates let non-designers quickly create professional-looking presentations and programs. Most of these programs provide the capability of creating hypertext links and jumps that let users choose which information to view and in what order they wish to view that information. Some of them let you create hot spots that can be clicked on with the mouse to jump to another topic. With some of the programs, the hot spot can be a graphic (including scanned images).

These 35mm slides were scanned and placed in the Macromedia Director 5.0 multimedia authoring program to create a travel presentation.

Scanning for Desktop Digital Video

Apple's QuickTime and Microsoft's Video for Windows digital video software lets you produce movies using your desktop personal computer. The movies you produce can be shown on your computer screen or transferred to videotape for playback with a Video Cassette Recorder (VCR).

Video capture boards are available for both Macintosh and IBM-compatible PCs to let you copy videos from a VCR or video camera onto your computer's hard disk where they can be edited with video editing programs such as Adobe Premiere (available on both Mac and Windows). With software such as Premiere, you can arrange the video clips into any order you choose. You can add titles to your movies and create special effects such as fade-in and fade-out.

This 35mm slide was scanned as a TIFF file and imported into Adobe Premiere and inserted into a digital movie. The single scanned image was then duplicated to create additional digital video frames.

Light and Color

These illustrations are described in Chapter 1.

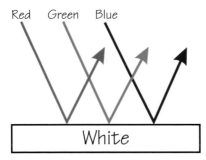

Figure 1
An object appears white to the human eye and to photographic film because all of the light striking the object is reflected (all of the red, green, and blue).

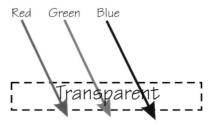
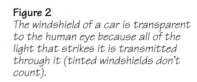

Figure 2
The windshield of a car is transparent to the human eye because all of the light that strikes it is transmitted through it (tinted windshields don't count).

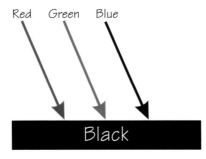

Figure 3
This object appears black to the human eye and to photographic film because all of the light striking the object is absorbed.

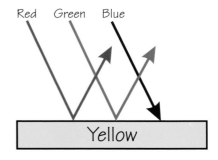

Figure 4
This object appears yellow to the human eye and to photographic film because the blue component of white light is absorbed while the red and green, which combine to produce yellow, are reflected.

Color Models

These illustrations are described in Chapter 1.

Additive Color (RGB)

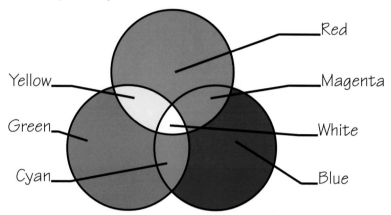

Figure 5
When two of the primary colors are combined, they produce one of the secondary colors. For example, red and green combined produce yellow. When all three primary colors are combined they produce white.

Subtractive Color (CMK)

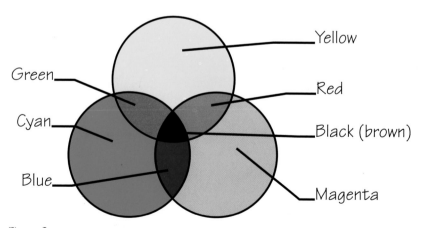

Figure 6
When two of the secondary colors are combined, they produce one of the primary colors. For example, yellow and cyan combined produce green. When all three subtractive secondary colors are combined they produce black.

These illustrations are described in Chapter 1.

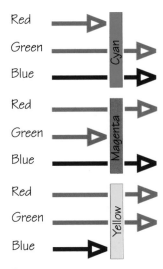

Figure 7

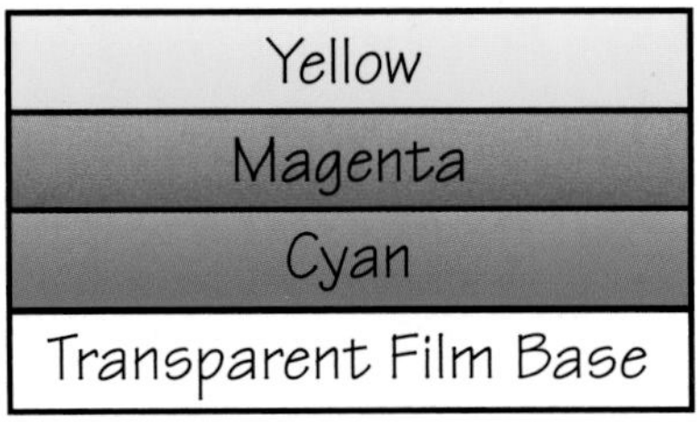

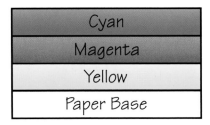

Figure 8
The dye layers in photographic negatives and positive transparencies.

Figure 9
The dye layers in photographic paper prints

These illustrations are described in Chapter 1.

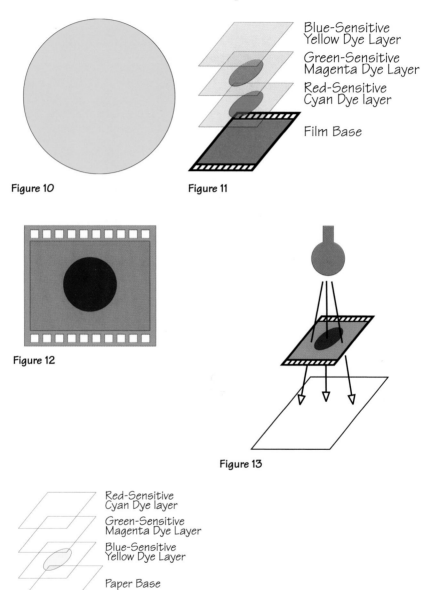

Figure 10

Figure 11

Blue-Sensitive
Yellow Dye Layer

Green-Sensitive
Magenta Dye Layer

Red-Sensitive
Cyan Dye layer

Film Base

Figure 12

Figure 13

Red-Sensitive
Cyan Dye layer

Green-Sensitive
Magenta Dye Layer

Blue-Sensitive
Yellow Dye Layer

Paper Base

Figure 14

Color Photo Examples

These photographs are described in Chapter 3.

Figure 15
Scanned as a color photo with 16 colors. File size: 80,294 bytes.

Figure 16
Scanned as a color photo with 256 colors. File size: 161,734 bytes.

Figure 17
Scanned as a color photo with millions of colors. File size: 480,204.

Color Photo File Size Example

This photograph appears in black-and-white in Chapter 4.

Figure 18
This photograph was scanned as a Sharp Millions of Colors Photograph at 200 ppi and saved in each of the file formats used by your HP ScanJet scanner. Refer to the color photo example in Chapter 4 for a chart showing the file sizes of each of the file formats.

JPEG File Examples

These photographs are described in Chapter 4.

Figure 19
Scanned as a TIFF file at 300 ppi. File size: 1,675,924 bytes.

Figure 20
JPEG file saved with low quality. File size: 18,988 bytes.

Figure 21
JPEG file saved with medium quality. File size: 170,640 bytes.

Figure 22
JPEG file saved with maximum quality. File size: 628,804 bytes.

GIF Examples

These photographs are described in Chapter 4.

Figure 23
TIFF file scanned at 200 ppi with millions of colors.

Figure 24
Indexed color image exported with the GIF89a filter using eight colors. File size: 83,632.

Figure 25
Indexed color image exported with the GIF89a filter using 64 colors. File size: 197,687.

Figure 26
Indexed color image exported with the GIF89a filter using 256 colors. File size: 279,413.

Color Adjustments

These photographs appear in Chapter 5.

Figure 27
The color in this photo is too red because of the early morning light.

Figure 28
In this example, the excessive red color has been removed with the Color Adjustment tool.

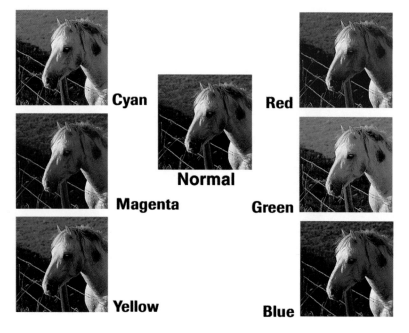

Figure 29
Examples of changes to the color hue made with the HP DeskScan II Color Adjustment tool.

Image Editor Examples

The techniques used on these photographs are explained in Chapter 6.

Figure 30
A 35 mm slide scanned into Adobe Photoshop with the transparency adapter using TWAIN .

Figure 31
The same image shown on the left after Kai's Power Tools 3.0 Gradient Filter was applied to the selected background.

Figure 32
A 35 mm slide scanned into Adobe Photoshop with the transparency adapter using TWAIN .

Figure 33
You can turn day into night! The background was selected and filled with black. The Adobe Photoshop Lens Flare filter was then applied to the background.

Clip Art Examples

These examples are explained in detail in Chapter 9.

Figure 34

Figure 35

Plug-in Filter Examples

Following are examples of several Adobe Photoshop plug-in filters applied to the same scanned image. The image was scanned from a color photographic print at 200 ppi. I selected the sky background with Photoshop's Magic Wand tool, then applied the various filters to the selected area. Plug-in filters are described in detail in Chapter 9.

Figure 36
Kai's Power Tools Gradient Designer filter was applied to the selected background.

Figure 37
Adobe Photoshop's Gradient Tool Copper radial fill was applied to the selected background. Next, Kai's Power Tools Spheroid Designer filter was applied to the same area.

Figure 38
Alien Skin's Eye Candy Glass filter was applied to the selected background.

Figure 39
The selected background was first filled with green. Alien Skin's Eye Candy Weave filter was then applied to the selected background.

You can use still photographs, drawings, and illustrations (including those scanned with your HP ScanJet) in your digital videos. Still images can be used as backgrounds for titles; or by using a technique called an *insert*, you can place a still image in a frame on top of a moving image.

How to Scan Images for Digital Video

Images scanned with your HP ScanJet color scanner can be imported into video editing programs such as Adobe Premiere. You can scan the images for digital video in one of a number of file formats including:

- PCX*
- TIFF*
- Windows Bitmap* (BMP)
- Macintosh PICT*
- Targa
- Adobe Photoshop

The file formats marked with an asterisk* are directly supported by the HP DeskScan II software. The other file formats can be used by scanning with TWAIN into an image editor such as Adobe Photoshop or Corel PHOTO-PAINT.

If you don't remember all the good information I gave you on file formats in Chapter 4, it is okay to go back for a review. But next time, there will be a test (just joking).

Images scanned for digital video should be scanned at the size of the digital video frame. For example, if your digital video frame size is 160 x 120 pixels (the standard size for most desktop video), you should scan your image at the same size (160 x 120 pixels). Apple QuickTime and Microsoft Video for Windows have standard video frame sizes: normally 160 x 120, 240 x 180, 360 x 240, or 640 x 480. Some video capture systems can create full-screen, full motion video clips. Scanning an image at a size that is different from the size used for the video wastes disk space and may cause jagged images on the screen.

Don't scan images for digital video at a higher resolution than 72 ppi. Scanning at higher resolutions doesn't give you a better image on the computer screen and needlessly takes up disk space.

Online Help Documentation

*B*oth Macintosh and Windows software programs normally include online help files or help documentation. Until recently, most of these help files were text-only. As software has become more graphical, the online help has of necessity become more graphical. Most online help now includes graphics. These graphics can be simple illustrations or drawings, graphics of the software screens, and some online help now includes scanned images. The scanned images can be scans of drawings or photographs. As the online help files are normally copied to the user's hard disk, you can't go overboard on the number of graphics or the resolution. As the images are normally used for display on the computer screen only, they do not have to have a resolution higher than 72 to 96 ppi. In most cases, you also do not need more than 256 colors. Guidelines for the development of online help systems are available from Apple Computer and from Microsoft.

Scanning for the World Wide Web, Online Services, and Bulletin Boards

*I*nexpensive, high-speed computer modems have spurred a tremendous growth in computer Bulletin Board Systems (BBSs), computer information services such as CompuServe, Prodigy, America Online, and of course the World Wide Web on the Internet. In the early days of the personal computer revolution, computer modems were slow and expensive. Modems were used primarily to transmit and receive text. The cost and time required to transmit graphics were too great. Now it is possible to rapidly transmit and receive not only text, but full-color graphic images. With the development of the Internet's information highway, distribution of newsletters, product information, technical bulletins, and even complete magazines is possible. Just as most people are not satisfied with text-only printed publications, they will not be satisfied with text-only electronic documents and publications. If you wish to communicate effectively in this new era of paperless communication, you will need a method of incorporating graphics into your online publications. Your HP ScanJet color scanner provides the perfect tool for going graphical on the information highway.

In this example, I scanned a 35mm slide with TWAIN and saved it as a GIF file to send to my son in New Jersey via CompuServe on the Internet.

The World Wide Web, computer bulletin boards, and information services are being used to upload and download information for business, public, and private use. Businesses are using BBSs and information services to provide product information, service instructions, and to exchange reports and data. Governmental and public sector service organizations are using these systems to distribute information on such topics as missing children, public policy issues, pollution problems, etc. Several missing children organizations are using computer information systems to distribute data, including photographs, of the missing children. Medical facilities are using the same methods to exchange medical charts and photographs, including x-rays.

The growth of the Internet and World Wide Web has been nothing short of phenomenal. It seems like everyone who is anyone has (or will have) a home page on the Web. People have even created home pages for cats and dogs (yes, it is true).

Home page of a fictitious railroad club displayed using the Spry Mosaic browser. The picture was scanned into Adobe Photoshop from DeskScan using TWAIN and saved as a 72 ppi GIF file.

Scanning for Documentation Management

*D*ocument management is a process of scanning documents (the entire page) and using specialized software called Desktop Document Management (DDM) to store, retrieve, and manage the resulting files. Document management systems are being used to replace microfilm and other processes that utilize photographic film. Documents that are scanned with DDM software can include both text and graphics. The documents are normally stored as bitmapped images, so the text cannot be edited. Some DDM software programs include OCR capabilities that let you convert the text from a bitmapped image to text that can be edited.

Some of the programs include database management capabilities that allow you to search for documents with keyword searches. Some of the programs include the capability to fax documents or to transmit them with email.

Combining your HP ScanJet scanner, desktop management software, and a CDR writer will give you a very powerful document storage and retrieval system that can be used to replace paper storage of a large number of documents.

Scanning for CD-ROMs and CDRs

*C*D-ROM stands for *Compact Disc-Read-Only Memory*. It is a technical term for what is essentially the same type of compact disc that you use to play your favorite music on your CD player. The ROM part comes from the fact that CD-ROMS can only be read or played (read only memory) by CD-ROM drives. Data cannot be added to or deleted from these discs (special CD-ROM drives are available that let you create your own CD-ROMs). Each CD-ROM disc can hold about 600 megabytes of data. To save this much information to floppy disks would require that you have about 550 disks on-hand to insert into your computer.

CD-ROM drives are becoming increasing popular as a distribution medium and multimedia would be impossible without the mass storage capabilities they offer. Almost all new PCs come with a built-in CD-ROM drive. CD-ROMS are being used for multimedia programs including digital video. They are being used to store large database files. And, they are being used to store graphical images such as clip art and photographs that do not fit onto normal 1.44 megabyte floppy disks. A CD-ROM provides an excellent storage medium for your scanned images. You do not have to be concerned about keeping your scanned files smaller than 1.44 megs and you do not have to use file compression unless you wish to store large numbers of scanned files.

Until recently, the production of CD-ROMs was limited to large production facilities who produced glass CD masters that were used to produce many duplicates. The cost to produce a master in this manner is about $2,000, with each duplicate costing from about $1.35 to $2.00, depending upon the number of copies.

It is now technically and financially possible to produce your own CD-ROMs using a compact disk writer (abbreviated CDR). Until recently, the price of a CDR recorder was in the $6,000 to $10,000 range. CDR recorders are now available for under $1,000.

You can use a CDR recorder to produce photo CDs, archive large numbers of scanned images, send scanned images to commercial printers, and in any situation where you have a large number of files or images with high resolution that occupy large amounts of space.

The discs produced by CDR writers can be read by most CD-ROM drives, but the discs are not the same. You cannot write to a CD-ROM disc, only to writable CDR discs. You cannot, in most cases, produce a CDR disc by simply copying files to the disc. You must use special CD writing software to organize the files and to format the disc.

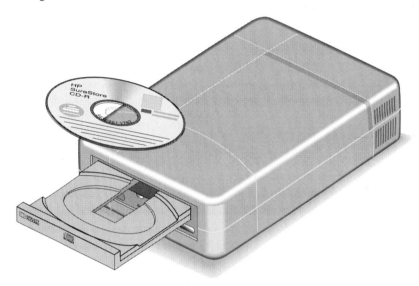

The Hewlett-Packard SureStore 6020 CD-Writer. Shown is the external model that can be used with Macs and PCs. The 6020 is also available as an internal model that fits inside Intel PCs (the internal model does not work with a Mac).

Tips for Scanning Images for the Screen

When preparing to scan images for the Web or online information services, there are several things to consider:

- What file formats are normally used on the Web, BBSs, and online information systems ?
- What resolution number should you use?
- What file formats display best on a computer screen?
- What file formats require the least disk space?
- What is the best image type for screen display?

What File Formats Should I Use for Online?

In most cases, file size is of prime importance when uploading or down-loading files from computer bulletin boards or online information systems. *Uploading* means you transmit a file to the bulletin board or online service, *downloading* means a file is sent from the BBS or online service to you. Large files translate to long transmission times and in-creased fees. When scanning images for transmission by modem, it is important to create the smallest appropriate file size. An important part of creating small files for transmission is the selection of the file format.

Should I Use GIF or JPEG?

If you are going to be uploading a file to an online service or if you are creating your own home page on the World Wide Web, you will probably want to include scanned images. You have probably heard that you should use either GIF or JPEG as your file format. Which one is best?

Currently, the most widely used file format on computer bulletin boards and online informa-tion services is *GIF* (Graphics Interchange Format). GIF files cannot have more than 256 colors or shades of gray. Your HP ScanJet color scanner cannot directly produce GIF files, but if you use TWAIN with one of the image editors, you can save the scanned image in the GIF format. At the time of this book's publication, GIF was being replaced by the PNG format because of legal problems relating to patents.

The second most widely used format for images on the Web, bulletin boards, and online services is JPEG. JPEG is an abbreviation of *Joint Photographic Experts Group* (the group that developed the standard). JPEG uses a "lossy" compression method, which means your image will lose some quality when it is compressed. This usually is not a problem for images that are displayed on a computer screen (it is more of a problem for images that are printed).

For more information on the GIF file format, refer to Page 57. For information on JPEG, refer to Page 53.

What Resolution Should I Use for Online Images?

Images that are for display on computer screens only and that will not be printed should be scanned at 72 to 95 ppi (this is the resolution of most computer screens). Scanning at a higher resolution simply wastes disk space and will increase your modem transmission times (and fees if you are using one of the online services such as CompuServe). If you are scanning to produce a file that will be transmitted to someone for printing, the same guidelines that normally apply to scanning resolution should be used.

HP DeskScan II has a print path already calibrated for images that are to be displayed on a computer screen (it is named "Screen"). If you use this print path, your images will be optimized for use on the Web, bulletin board, or online service.

What File Formats Require the Least Disk Space?

Of the two file formats normally used for files on the Web or online services, JPEG or GIF, JPEG produces the smaller file. To illustrate this, I scanned this image as a TIFF file (so I could print it here in the book) and also saved the same image as GIF and JPEG files.

In the TIFF format, the files was 642,318 bytes. As a GIF file, the same image was 23,338 bytes. When the image was saved as a JPEG file with medium compression, the file was only 8,612 bytes. When you save a file with an application that supports JPEG, you have several choices of file compression.

What Is the Best Image Type for Screen Display?

If you are scanning a photograph for display on the computer screen, use one of the DeskScan II photograph image types (Black-and-White or Color Photo). If you are scanning a color drawing, use Color Photo (don't use Color Drawing...you will get better results using Color Photo in this case). The only one of the halftone patterns that works for the screen is Diffusion.

Chapter 8

How to Trace
a Scanned Image

Introduction

*I*n this chapter I will describe the process of converting scanned bit-mapped images into drawings that can be modified with a drawing program such as Adobe Illustrator or CorelDRAW. Probably all of us used tracing paper to trace cartoons or photographs when we were in school. I can remember using a window as a light table and tracing my favorite cartoon characters (Terry and the Pirates, for those of you old enough to remember).

With drawing or tracing software and your HP ScanJet scanner, you can again trace sketches, drawings, or even photographs (but don't violate any copyrights).

Bitmap vs. Vector Graphics

*T*wo basic types of graphical images can be produced with a computer: bitmapped images and vector graphics. Each type has its advantages and disadvantages. It is possible to use your HP ScanJet scanner and specialized software to convert a bitmapped image to a vector graphic.

When you use your HP ScanJet scanner to scan a photograph or a drawing, the result is a bitmap. You can best visualize a bitmap if you think of it as a grid. The grid consists of rows of squares or pixels. The number of rows per square inch depends upon the resolution used to scan the image. Each pixel or square will be white, black, a shade of gray, or a color. Bitmapped images can be beautifully detailed reproductions of an original photograph or drawing, but they do have limitations.

Limitations of bitmapped images:

- Bitmapped images can require a large amount of disk space.
- Bitmapped images cannot be enlarged (scaled) very much without becoming jagged or fuzzy.
- Bitmapped images are fixed resolution (a 300 ppi bitmapped image will print at 300 ppi even if printed on a high-resolution output device such as an imagesetter).
- Bitmapped images can be difficult and time-consuming to edit with image editors or paint programs.

Benefits of vector graphics:

- A vector graphic can be enlarged or reduced in size (scaled) without losing detail or becoming jagged.

- A vector graphic prints at the highest resolution of the output device (the same vector graphic that prints at 300 dpi on a desktop printer will print at 1270 dpi or higher on a high resolution imagesetter).

- A vector graphic will occupy much less disk space than a bitmap of the same original.

What Is Tracing?

When you were young, did you ever place a sheet of tracing paper over a picture or drawing in a magazine or newspaper? Almost anyone who has ever done any kind of drawing or graphics has done some type of tracing. Tracing allows you to copy the essential parts of a photograph or drawing as the starting point for a new drawing. Professional graphic artists and illustrators have used the technique of tracing for years as part of their process of producing artwork and technical illustrations.

With traditional tracing methods, you place a sheet of semi-transparent paper (many types of specialized tracing papers are available in graphic arts supply stores) on top of a photograph, drawing, or other form of artwork and using a pen or pencil you draw lines that follow the parts of the original. Depending on how patient and careful you are, you can obtain a very accurate reproduction of the original.

When scanning or tracing any photograph, drawing, illustration, or any form of artwork, do not violate any copyrights or legal protections afforded to the creator of the original. It is a violation of U.S. and international copyright laws to reproduce or modify creative work produced by someone other than yourself without permission.

The traditional method of tracing using tracing paper, a light table, and pencils or pens is very time consuming and tedious. It is also very difficult to obtain identical results if you wish to repeat the process.

Today, with an HP ScanJet scanner and tracing or illustration software, you can scan a paper drawing, illustration, or photograph and electronically convert it to a vector graphic that can be edited or modified. The tracing or illustration software acts as electronic tracing paper.

Tracing Software

*I*n addition to your HP ScanJet scanner, you will need software to trace bitmapped images. You can use a drawing or illustration program such as Adobe Illustrator, Macromedia Freehand, or CorelDRAW that includes tracing capabilities, or you can use one of several specialized software programs that only perform tracing functions. The most popular and widely used of these are Adobe Streamline and Corel TRACE. Adobe Streamline is available for both Apple Macintosh and Windows systems, but Corel TRACE is only available for Windows.

Corel TRACE is not available separately, it is included with the CorelDRAW suite of software applications.

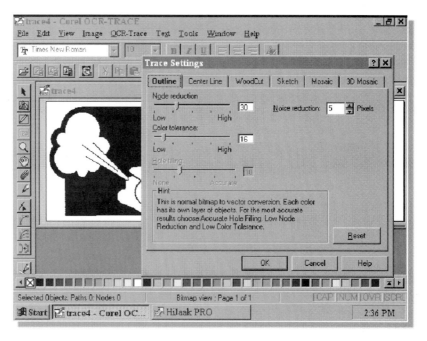

Corel TRACE OCR 6.0 functions as both a tracing program and OCR program. The OCR functions are not very elegant (or accurate), but if you only occasionally have need for OCR, they may be sufficient.

Tracing programs such as Adobe Streamline and Corel TRACE perform automatic tracing, but draw and illustration programs usually offer both automatic and manual modes. With the manual mode, you must select each line or segment of the bitmapped image that is to be traced. This method is slower, but offers precise control of the process.

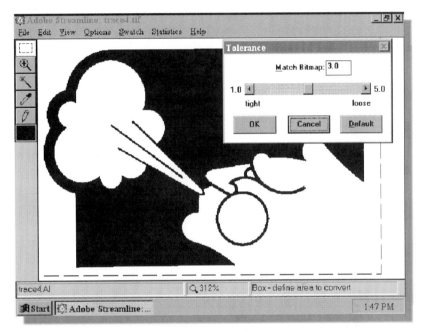

Adobe Streamline tracing software is available in both Macintosh and Windows versions (Windows version shown).

Tracing programs such as Adobe Streamline and Corel TRACE offer several options that control the tracing process and let you choose how your traced image will look. These options include:

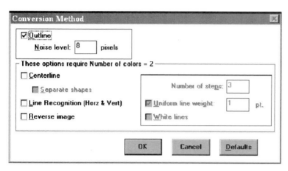

Conversion Method dialog box in Adobe Streamline.

■ **Conversion method**
This determines how the tracing program follows the lines in the bitmapped image. One choice lets you follow the outsides of the lines and the other method follows the centers of the lines. Conversion methods are fully described on Page 153.

■ **Tolerance**
This determines how closely the tracing program follows the bitmapped image. You usually have a choice of following the bitmap tightly (or closely) or loosely. The default is a point in between tight and loose.

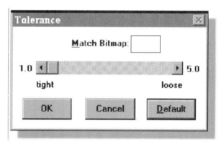

Tolerance option dialog box in Adobe Streamline.

Image traced with Adobe Streamline Tolerance option set to loose (maximum setting of 5).

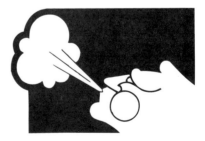

Image traced with Adobe Streamline Tolerance option set to tight (maximum setting of 1).

Tracing Line Art

*I*f you remember from Chapter 3, your HP ScanJet scanner recognizes six types of images. Two of those are black-and-white and color drawings. Drawings are also known as line art. This term comes from the techniques used to produce many of these drawings; that is, they are drawn with lines—hence *line art*. Line art does not always consist of just lines. Many times a drawing consists of lines and filled areas. Your HP ScanJet scanner combined with a drawing program or one of the tracing software programs will do an excellent job of tracing line art.

Conversion Methods

Most tracing software offers several tracing methods or options. The type of drawing you wish to trace or the effect you desire will determine which of the methods or options you use. Corel TRACE and Adobe Streamline offer two primary methods or options and Corel TRACE offers several additional specialty methods.

- **Outline**
  The tracing program traces the perimeter of a line or object.

- **Centerline**
  The tracing program traces the center of a line or object.

These two methods produce dramatically different results. The method you should use depends on the type of original and the effect that you wish to create in your tracing. Each method has its advantages and disadvantages. You may wish to experiment by tracing the same original using each method and compare the results.

The same original traced with the centerline method (left) and the outline method (right). In this particular example, the outline method produced a more accurate representation of the original.

Outline Method

The outline method works best with drawings that have filled areas such as clip art or pen-and-ink sketches. The outline method traces around the outline of an object then fills that object with black, white, or a color. The tracing will consist of a number of objects stacked on top of each other. Depending upon the complexity of the original, the tracing may consist of a large number of objects.

Clip art image traced with Adobe Streamline using the outline method.

The same image broken apart so you can see how it was traced. The image consists of separate shapes filled with white or black.

Centerline Method

The centerline method works best with originals that have no filled areas such as technical drawings, blueprints, etc. The centerline method traces the original by finding the center of the lines that make up the original. The tracing program makes the traced line equal to the width of the original line.

Clip art image traced using the centerline method. Note: Some lines are so thin, they don't show.

The same image broken apart so you can see how it was traced. I made the thin lines thicker so you could see them.

Tracing Photographs

*P*erhaps the most desired feature in a scanner among graphic artists and designers is the ability to trace photographs and convert them to line art. Line art technical illustrations are often preferred over photographs for technical documentation because details can be emphasized (or de-emphasized) in a drawing. Also, printing grayscale or color photographs requires the use of a better grade of paper than that of a line art drawing. However, it is very desirable to use a photograph as the starting point for producing a technical illustration. Illustrators and graphic artists have been manually tracing photographs for years as the starting point for their work.

Can a scanned photograph be traced and used in the same way as the manual method so favored by illustrators? The answer is yes, well maybe, and it depends. You can scan a color or grayscale photograph and trace it using one of the tracing programs, or you can import it into one of the drawing or illustration programs and trace it manually. The results you obtain will depend on the effect you want and on the complexity of the original photograph. When tracing a photograph, often there is too much detail and information for the tracing program to process. Even if the program can trace the image, the result may be so complex that it will not print and may be difficult if not impossible to edit. Tracing software is designed to search for the edges of lines or segments and a color or grayscale photograph may not have well-defined edges or segments. Sometimes, you can overcome this limitation by importing the scanned image into a drawing or illustration program and tracing the image manually. If the effect you wish to obtain is a technical line art illustration from the photograph, you may have to trace the photograph using a light table and conventional tracing paper. Then you will have to scan the tracing and use the tracing software to trace the scanned traced image. This may seem like a lot of effort, but it may be the only way to convert a photograph to a line art illustration and may be a lot less effort than drawing from scratch.

In most cases, tracing a photograph produces a posterization effect. This may be an acceptable outcome and may, in fact, be the result you wished to obtain. The following examples illustrate the posterization effect that results from tracing a grayscale photograph with a limited number of shades of gray. You can obtain better results by increasing the number of shades of gray, but you then increase the complexity of the resulting scan. The following examples illustrate tracing with 4 and 8 shades of gray. In this example, increasing the number of shades of gray to 16 produced an image that was so complex that it would not print on an HP LaserJet equipped with 8 megabytes of memory.

Photograph scanned at 200 ppi and saved as a TIFF file.

Photo traced with Adobe Streamline using 4 shades of gray. Resulting image contains 395 paths and 2731 nodes.

Photo traced with Adobe Streamline using 8 shades of gray. Resulting image contains 788 paths and 4050 nodes.

The Tracing Process

*T*he tracing process normally requires the use of several software programs. No single program does everything necessary to obtain a good traced image. Scanning software is necessary to scan the image. Often, you must use an image editor to remove unwanted details or to correct minor defects in the scanned image. You will need tracing software or an illustration program that offers tracing capabilities. And finally, you may require a drawing or illustration program to edit the vector graphic produced by the tracing process.

The following example illustrates a typical tracing session. The steps may vary if you use different software than what is show here. The tracing process begins with the selection of an original (sketch, drawing, blueprint, etc.). The better the original—the better the tracing.

1. Use HP DeskScan II to scan the original artwork to produce a bitmapped image. Select only the parts of the preview image that you want to be in your final scan to minimize the need to edit the bitmapped image. Use the lasso tool if necessary to select non-rectangular areas.

Tip

You may use HP DeskScan directly, or you may use TWAIN to scan the image into your image editor.

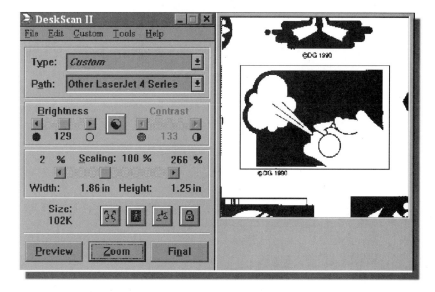

2. If necessary, load the scanned image into your image editor to delete unnecessary details or to straighten jagged lines.

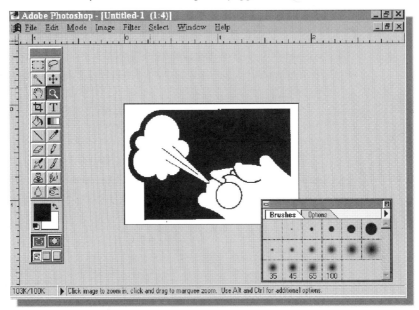

3. Start your tracing program and load the bitmapped image. Select the appropriate options and begin the trace.

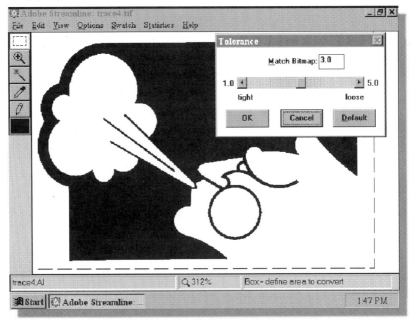

4. Save the traced image in one of the available vector graphic formats.

5. If necessary, load the traced image into your drawing or illustration program and edit the lines or segments.

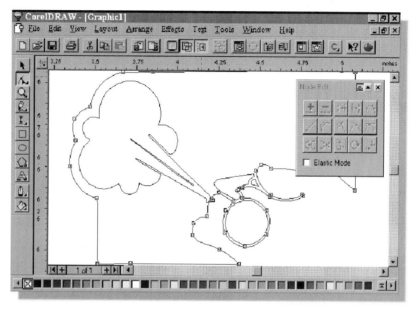

Tracing Tips

*T*he following tips will assist you in getting the best results when tracing line art.

- **Start with a good original.**
  If possible, select line art that is not physically damaged. Avoid line art that is faded or stained.

- **Scan at the highest optical (not interpolated) resolution of the scanner.**
  You will get a better tracing from a higher resolution bitmap.

- **Scan at a lower brightness level.**
  Line art with very thin lines usually scans better with a lower brightness level. But, don't lower the brightness too much. You may get "background noise" from the paper (artifacts).

- **Don't trace text.**
  If you need text in your final drawing, it is better to remove the text from the bitmapped image prior to tracing and put it back in with the text tools in your drawing or illustration program. An exception to this tip would be if the original drawing has text

that is in a typeface that you do not have and you wish to retain the text effect.

If you wish to scan text and convert it to editable text, use OCR software. See Page 127 for a description of OCR.

■ **Protect the original.**
If the original is rare or valuable, place acetate over it before scanning. The acetate also will help to thicken the lines by diffusing the image, which makes the scanner think the lines are somewhat thicker.

Special Effects with Tracing Software

*C*orel TRACE 6.0 (the current version at the time this book was written) includes several special effects capabilities that you can use to create drawings that are truly different. These special effects include:

■ **Wood Cut**
The image is traced using parallel lines of varying width.

■ **Sketch**
The image is traced using a mesh-like effect created by layers of parallel lines at different angles. You can control the number of layers to create different effects.

■ **Mosaic**
The image is traced using tiles of symmetrical objects (squares, circles). The number of objects can be controlled to create a more or less realistic effect.

■ **3D Mosaic**
Produces an effect similar to Mosaic but with 3D textured effects.

Photo scanned at 200 ppi and saved as a TIFF file.

Traced with Corel TRACE 6.0 using the Wood Cut special effects option.

Traced with Corel TRACE 6.0 using the Sketch special effects option.

Each of the trace options available with Corel TRACE offer a number of settings that allow you to customize the tracing process to suit your design requirements and your artistic persuasion.

Limitations of the Tracing Process

*U*sing your HP ScanJet scanner and one of the drawing or tracing programs to convert bitmapped images to vector drawings can produce some remarkable results and the process can be a real productivity enhancer; however, there are limitations to the tracing process:

■ **The process is not completely automatic.**

Often, you must edit the tracing with your drawing or illustration program to correct defects. The current releases of tracing software can produce accurate straight lines or accurate curves, but often cannot do both simultaneously. Sometimes the software makes a line that should have been straight into a curve, or vice versa. You may find it necessary to rework some of the lines. Experimentation with the software's tracing options may be necessary to determine the appropriate combination of settings that will produce a tracing that requires a minimum of editing.

■ Tracings sometimes are too complex to print.

If you are tracing a very complex original and if you set the tracing options to close tolerances, the resulting tracing may have so many segments, nodes, or lines that your printer may not have enough memory to print the tracing. Sometimes this can be overcome by reducing the tolerance level. In Adobe Streamline, this is called the Smooth Path command and it reduces the number of points in the drawing while attempting to retain the shape of the original.

Consult the user guide of your tracing or drawing program for more information on the various options and control settings.

Be prepared to experiment with your tracing or illustration software and be prepared to be frustrated sometimes. Tracing is an art as much as a science and you may not always be able to obtain the exact effect you wish. You may find that you must extensively edit the resulting traced image with your illustration or drawing program. Tracing photographs especially can be disappointing. Only you can determine if the results obtained are worth the effort required.

Chapter 9

How to...
Scanning Tips and Techniques

Introduction

*T*his is the "fun" chapter. This is where I get to share with you all of the creative and sometimes crazy techniques and tips that I have learned by playing around or that others have shared with me. Your HP ScanJet scanner is a very capable and professional tool. It can also be a heck of a lot of fun!

In this chapter I will show you how to do things with your scanner that perhaps you never thought of or never thought of doing "that" way. You can do things with and to your images that will amaze your friends and may even amaze you. I will tell you about using filters with your image editor to produce beautiful, interesting, weird, and wonderful effects. You may never have thought of your HP ScanJet scanner as a camera, but I will show you how you can scan "real" objects such as combs, paper clips, and other everyday objects and make them part of your newsletters, documents, or other projects.

Scanning a Photographic Proof Sheet

*A*photographic proof sheet (photographers also call them contact sheets or simply contacts) is a photographic print of a group of negatives produced by placing a sheet of photographic paper (usually 8x10 inches, but they can be larger or smaller) directly in contact with the negatives during the printing process. The photos on a proof sheet are exactly the same size as the negatives. A sheet of 8x10 inch photographic

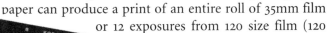

paper can produce a print of an entire roll of 35mm film or 12 exposures from 120 size film (120 film is known as medium format and negatives on this format can be 6x6 cm, 6x4.5 cm, or 6x7 cm). Photographic proof sheets can be color or black-and-white and can be made from color negatives, black-and-white negatives, or positive proof sheets can be made from color transparencies (35mm slides, medium format, or large-sized transparencies).

Proof sheets are used by photographers, graphic designers, and magazine and newspaper editors to preview negatives prior to producing enlargements. They use the sheets to determine if the negatives are in sharp focus, have correct exposure, and to determine which negative caught the appropriate action or mood. It is time-consuming and costly to produce enlargements of each nega-

A scan of the proof sheet shown on the previous page. This image was scaled 250 percent, the resolution increased to 250 ppi, and maximum sharpening was applied. While the image is useful for positioning and editorial reviews, compare the quality to the scan made of the enlargement (shown below).

tive, so using the contact sheets saves time and money. Proof sheets are also used to indicate which portions of the negative should be printed (photographers call this process *cropping*).

A scan from a 5x7 inch enlargement of the same negative shown above. Note the improvement in quality. Scanning from a proof sheet is a temporary way of including images in drafts and reviews, but it cannot be used to replace the scanning of enlargements.

You can use a proof sheet and your HP ScanJet scanner to produce temporary scans of selected negatives while waiting for the photo lab to produce quality enlargements that you can scan later to replace the temporary scans. Photographers and publishers refer to this process as FPO (*For Position Only*). These FPO scans can be placed in your documents temporarily so that reviewers and editors can see what the final layout and content will look like.

How to Scan a Photo Proof Sheet

1. Place the proof sheet either horizontally or vertically on the scanner glass depending on the orientation of the particular negative that you want to scan.

2. Click on the **Preview** button.

3. Use the marquee tool (also called a selection rectangle) to select the particular negative you want to use.

4. Use the **Scaling** slider bar to enlarge the image until the width and height are the size you desire (make sure you have selected uniform scaling).

5. Increase the resolution by referring to one of the charts on Pages 109-110.

6. Scan your selection with Sharpening set to **Extra Heavy**.

Refer to Page 78 for information on scaling and to Page 92 for information on sharpening.

When you get an enlargement from a photo lab and scan it, use the same file name that you used for your temporary FPO scan and it will automatically replace the temporary scan in your document.

It might be helpful for the photo lab producing your enlargements to give them a print of your document with the temporary scanned image so they can see how you plan to use it. Indicate to the photo lab that you plan to scan the enlargement and they should know how to produce the best print for scanning (if they don't, go to a different lab). If you cropped the image the way you wanted the enlargement to look, simply tell them to print it this way! If you didn't crop it the way you wanted during scanning, you can use a pen or marker to annotate the print of the document to show the lab which parts you want. It is better to have the photo lab make the enlargement the way you plan to use it rather than cropping later. If they print it the way you plan to use it, you can reduce the amount of cropping and enlarging or reducing you will have to do during scanning.

Scanning Photographic Negatives

*I*f you purchased a Transparency Adapter with your HP ScanJet IIcx, 3c, or 4c, you can use it to scan black-and-white photographic negatives to produce inexpensive contact or proof sheets. Then you can scan negatives to use as FPO placeholders until you get prints of the negatives made by a photo lab.

Scanning photographic negatives with the transparency adapter has a number of limitations that you should be aware of.

- You cannot scan color negatives (the process of inverting the image from negative to positive will not give acceptable results with color negatives).

- Scanning black-and-white negatives to use as proof sheets or FPO is possible, but the resulting images may suffer from posterization effects.

- The proof sheets you produce by scanning negatives can be useful for determining the content of your rolls or sheets of film, but they will not be as useful as a proof sheet made on photographic paper for determining focus (because of the limited resolution of laser printers compared to the resolution of a photographic print).

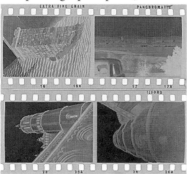

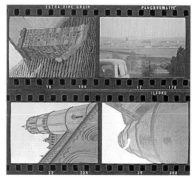

Black-and-white 35mm negatives scanned directly with the ScanJet Transparency Adapter.

The same image after being inverted to produce a positive image.

You can scan an individual negative, scale it to the desired size, and use it temporarily in your document. When scanning 35mm negatives, be sure to use maximum sharpening and set the resolution to match the scaling percentage using the charts on Pages 109-110 to determine the correct resolution. You will get better results from larger negatives such as those used in medium or large format cameras. Typically the negatives produced by these cameras are 2-1⁄4 x 2-1⁄4 to 4x5 inches in size and will not require the same amount of image scaling as 35mm film. You will also get better results by manipulating the scanned image with an image editor. Usually after inverting the image from negative to positive, you will have to adjust the image contrast and density. It is possible to scan a negative and produce images that you can use temporarily, but you will get much better results by having a paper print made by a photo lab and using the print for your scans.

A 35mm negative scanned with the Transparency Adapter. Image was scaled 250% and given maximum sharpening. The resolution was increased to 350 ppi.

The same image shown on the left copied and inverted in Adobe Photoshop. The inverted image was darkened and the contrast increased slightly. Note the posterization effect in the sky portion of the image.

How to Scan a Negative

To scan a negative correctly, it must be placed on the scanner glass with the emulsion side of the film up (away from the glass). If you place the film on the glass incorrectly, your image will be backwards. The film emulsion is the side of the film that is coated with silver. It is where the image is recorded. There are several methods for recognizing the emulsion side of film:

■ Film normally has a slight curl to it. The emulsion side is always on the inside of the curl. The base side is always on the outside.

- One side of the film will be dull; this is the emulsion side. The other side will be shiny; this is called the base side.

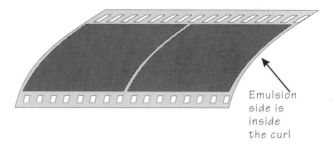

Emulsion side is inside the curl

The emulsion side of the film is always on the inside of the film curl. The base (or shiny) side is on the outside of the film curl.

- Another way of recognizing the emulsion side is to look at the text printed on the film. If you can read the text, you are looking at the base (shiny) side of the film; the emulsion (dull) side will be the other side.

When the emulsion side (dull) of the film is down or away from you and the base (or shiny side) is towards you, you can read the text on the film.

Modifying Scanned Images with an Image Editor

Some of your scanned images may not be perfect! The original photograph or drawing may have imperfections or defects such as scratches, dirt spots, cracks, or other physical defects. Sometimes mistakes were made during the shooting of the photograph, such as trees growing out a person's head or a distracting sign in the background. In most cases, it is not possible to shoot the photograph over again. Is it possible to remove or eliminate these defects and is it hard to do?

In professional photographic studios and on the staffs of professional publications, retouching specialists use airbrushes and other tools to retouch photographs. With your HP ScanJet scanner and one of the image editing programs such as Adobe Photoshop or Corel PHOTO-PAINT, you can perform similar modifications and retouching on your scanned images.

Let's see how this can be done by looking at a photograph that contains a distracting background. The photograph below of an antique steam locomotive would be much better if that electric utility pole in the background were not there. Since I couldn't cut it down and the location made it difficult to position the camera so that it wasn't in the background, let's see if we can remove it digitally.

Image editors such as Adobe Photoshop and Corel PHOTO-PAINT include many tools such as paintbrushes, pencils, airbrushes and erasers.

These tools enable you remove portions of an image and blend the deleted area into the rest of the image so that your audience will not be able to detect the modification.

To remove the offending electric utility pole, I used Adobe Photoshop's eyedropper, airbrush, and pencil tools. I first used the eyedropper tool to select a portion of the sky near the pole and then used the airbrush and pencil tools to paint over the offending area. The size of the airbrush,

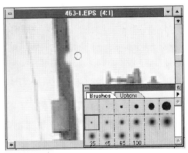

The airbrush tool is used here to paint over the utility pole. Used in combination with the eyedropper tool, I blended the removed portion into the existing background.

pencil, and paintbrush tools can be enlarged or reduced so that you can modify details as small as one pixel.

When using an image editor to modify or enhance your scanned images, you should make a copy of the image file and use the copy for your modifications so that if you make a serious mistake, you can always go back to your original file to begin again.

You can use the zoom tool to enlarge the image on your computer screen so that you can work on detail as small as a pixel. It takes a bit of experimentation and practice and you will probably make mistakes the first time you try it.

Let's see how I well I did. The ugly electric utility pole is gone. Too bad we can't remove graffiti and highway billboards this easily! Notice that in the process of removing the pole, I used the airbrush to add smoke to blend with the rest of the background.

Having Fun with Image Editor Filters

*P*hotographic filters are pieces of glass or gelatin placed on a camera lens to filter the light entering the lens. They are used to lighten or darken colors, or to add special effects, such as stars. Photographic filters can also be used as magnifying lenses and to polarize light. Image editor filters are actually computer programs that run inside of your image editing program. With these filters, you can duplicate some of the effects that you get with camera filters and you can produce effects that no camera filter can produce. You can have a lot of fun and produce some spectacular effects with your scanned images by using the filters in the image editing software.

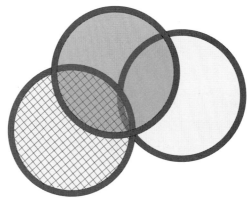

Photographic filters are usually made of glass and are attached to the front of a camera lens to lighten or darken colors or to produce special effects.

Image editing programs usually include a number of filters and some programs, such as Adobe Photoshop and Corel PHOTO-PAINT, allow you to add filters that can be purchased from other software companies. Adobe pioneered this concept and calls these filters *plug-ins*. The Adobe Photoshop plug-in concept has become somewhat of a standard and most filters are Photoshop-compatible. A number of companies have produced filter plug-ins and the number seems to increase almost daily.

Refer to Page 245 for a list of currently available Photoshop plug-in filters.

The original photograph with no filter effects applied.

Same photograph after the Adobe Photoshop cloud filter was applied to the background.

You can usually apply a filter to an entire image or to a selected portion of it. You can also combine filters. Some of the filter effects only work on color images, but most work on color and grayscale images.

Almost all of the Photoshop-compatible plug-in filters are available for both Macintosh and Windows systems. New filters are often introduced on one of the platforms first and on the other one a bit later. New filters are being developed regularly and it is difficult for a book such as this to have the latest information on filters.

Adobe Photoshop Gaussian Blur filter applied to the glass in the lamp.

Adobe Photoshop Gradient filter applied to the background of the image.

Refer to Page 243 for a list of publications that regularly cover products like Photoshop plug-in filters and scanning.

Kai's Power Tools

One of the most interesting and exciting sets of Photoshop plug-in filters is Kai's Power Tools (exciting effects and interesting user interface). Power Tools (abbreviated KPT) gives you the capability to add gradients, fractals, and textures in literally millions of possible combinations.

A gradient effect applied with Kai's Power Tools 3.0.

A texture effect applied with Kai's Power Tools 3.0.

Kai's Power Tool Page Curl Filter.

Page Curl effect applied with Kai's Page Curl Filter.

One of the most interesting parts of the KPT set is called the Lens f/x. The user interface is unusual, to say the least. The tool can be placed anywhere on the screen. A preview opening lets you see the filter effect applied to your image. The tools around the edges let you control the intensity and opacity of the image, the direction of the effect, and various options.

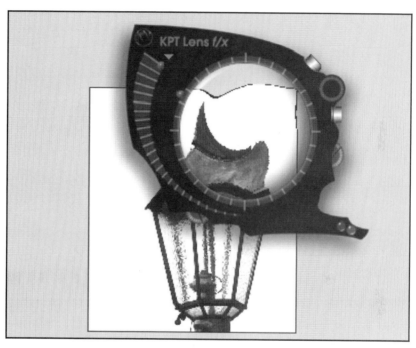

KPT Lens f/x filter being used to apply a twirl effect to the scanned image.

Resultant twirl effect applied with the Lens f/x filter.

Spheres applied with the Spheroid Designer in Kai's Power Tools.

Eye Candy Filters

Another interesting and very useful set of Photoshop plug-in filters is Eye Candy, which is available from Alien Skin Software (not joking, that's their real name…great folks). Producing drop shadows is an effect that many like, but is a time-consuming and not easily duplicated process. Eye Candy includes a drop shadow filter that makes the process almost automatic.

In this first example, I applied the Eye Candy Drop Shadow filter to the image with the cloud background.

Here I applied the Outer Bevel filter to the entire image.

Eye Candy also includes filters for creating cutouts, inner and outer bevels, carves, motion trails, glass effects, swirls, chrome, smoke, water drops, weave effects, and HSB noise.

In this example, I filled the background with black, selected the lamp, and applied the Glow filter.

Here I selected the background, filled it with light gray, and applied the Swirl filter.

The Eye Candy filters are unique among image editing filters in that some of their effects are created on the outside of the selection area. That is how it is possible to so easily create drop shadows, glow, motion trail, and outer bevel effects. Each of the filters offers many options and a preview window.

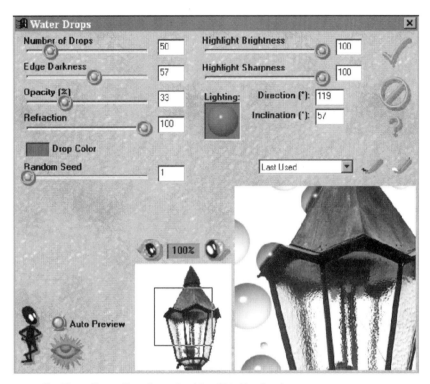

The Water Drops filter from the Alien Skin Eye Candy set.

Eye Candy Cutout filter effect applied to selected text that was added to the scanned image.

Andromeda Series Filters

Andromeda Software produces three series of Adobe Photoshop plug-in filters. Series 1 provides a number of effects such as multiple images, stars, etc. Series 2 lets you place your images onto the surfaces of cubes, cylinders, planes, or spheres. Series 3 filters provide Mezzotint effects.

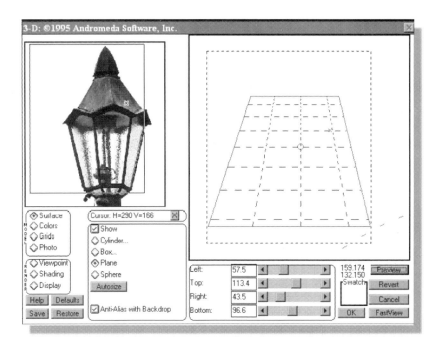

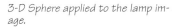

3-D Sphere applied to the lamp image.

3-D Plane applied to the lamp image.

KPT Convolver

This plug-in filter set is made by the same folks (MetaTools) who produce Kai's Power Tools. Convolver is hard to describe. It has a very interesting (some would say weird) user interface (see illustration below). KPT Convolver offers limitless options for sharpen, blur, emboss, and other effects.

KPT Convolver effect applied to the selected lamp. Background filled with black.

Two filters applied to one image. KPT Power Tools texture applied to background. KPT Convolver effect applied to the lamp.

Adobe Gallery Effects

These filters were originally produced by Aldus and are now marketed by Adobe. There are three volumes in the set. When first introduced, the filters were not Photoshop plug-ins, but they have since been upgraded to include this capability. These filters are now included with Adobe Photoshop 4.0. Each volume includes 17 filters and each filter has a control panel that lets you customize settings to produce almost unlimited variations.

Crosshatch filter applied to the selected lamp.

Reticulation filter applied to the selected background.

Craquelure filter applied to the selected background.

Halftone Screen applied to the selected background.

Auto F/X Photo/Graphic Edges

This filter set consists of two volumes of over 1500 different edge effects that you can apply to your scanned images. Volume I contains over 750 traditional edge effects including artistic, deckled, translucent, and darkroom-type effects. Volume II contains over 750 geometric and unique digital edge effects.

Each effect consists of a 400 ppi TIFF file that you can resize to match your scanned photo in an image editor such as Adobe Photoshop or Corel PHOTO-PAINT. Each effect includes a selection area that masks your scanned image. You load both images at the same time and copy your scanned image to the clipboard. Then you paste your image into the selection and it is masked inside the edge effect.

This type of effect can be very difficult and time-consuming to create manually within your image editor. In some cases, you might not be able to create the effect yourself. Each volume includes so many different effects, you would have to scan a lot of images before you had to use an effect for a second time.

Auto F/X Photo/Graphic edge filter applied to a grayscale scanned image.

Adding Text to Scanned Images

*I*t has been said for years that "a picture is worth a thousand words." I think this is true in some cases, but communications that combine graphics with text can be more powerful than the two alone. You can add text to your scanned images in several ways. You can add text directly to the scanned image with an image editor. You can import scanned images into a drawing or illustration program and make the scanned image part of the drawing. You can import a scanned image into a desktop publishing program and use that program's text tools to place text on top of the scanned image.

Text added to scanned image with Adobe Photoshop. Text was placed on a separate layer and made semi-transparent.

Each of these methods offers advantages and disadvantages. Perhaps the easiest method is to add text with your image editor. The text becomes part of the image and moves with the image. The disadvantage of this method is that once the text is added to the bitmapped image, it can no longer be edited as text.

Importing a scanned image into an illustration or drawing program offers the advantage of keeping the text and image separate. You can still edit the text as text. A disadvantage of this method is that you cannot apply some of the wonderful image editor filter effects to the text.

Importing a scanned image into a DTP program or word processing program and adding text on the scanned image offers the advantage of having editable text, but the disadvantage of not being able to use the filter effect as well as the logistics of keeping the image and text together. Some programs let you link the image and text and some do not.

Text added to scanned image with Adobe Photoshop. Glow effect applied to selected text with Alien Skin Eye Candy filter.

You can use your image editor to add text to your scanned images to create exciting effects. Most image editors now have layer features that let you place text on one layer and your scanned image on another. You can use this feature to make the text or the image transparent or semi-transparent. You can also use the image editor's filter effects on the text or the image for even more interesting and creative effects.

Text added to scanned image with Adobe Photoshop. Effect applied to selected text with Eye Candy Carve filter.

Manipulating Your Images

You can do many interesting, exciting, and creative things with your scanned images, image editor, and illustration program. You can create montages, mask an image so that it shows through text or another image, and you can fade one image into another.

One scanned image faded into another using Adobe Photoshop's layer and mask features. Thanks to Craig Swanson's Photoshop Techniques Issue Number 22 for this technique.

Scanned images can be imported into illustration and drawing programs and combined with vector drawings to create interesting and unusual combinations.

The text was converted to a mask on a layer in Adobe Photoshop. The text was made transparent so the image could show through. Alien Skin's Eye Candy Shadow filter was used to add a drop shadow behind the text.

How to Use Your Scanner as a Camera

*I*n Chapter 2, *How Color Scanning Works*, I compared a scanner to a camera. Well now I can tell you the rest of the story. Your scanner can "be a camera." You can use your HP ScanJet color scanner to scan real, 3-D, physical objects. There are some limitations, of course, but your scanner makes a pretty good camera. Obviously, you are limited to scanning objects that can fit onto the glass (without breaking it of course). The objects also can only be about two inches thick. The scanner has a limited depth-of-focus (photographers call this depth-of-field). If you attempt to scan an object that is thicker than two inches, part of it will be in sharp focus and part will be unsharp or fuzzy. In some cases this will be okay as it places emphasis on the foreground part of the object.

Be very careful when scanning 3-D physical objects. You could break or scratch your scanner glass. Don't put anything heavy on the scanner or anything with a rough surface that might scratch the glass. If you must place something on the glass that has the potential to damage the glass, cover the glass with a sheet of clean, clear acetate. You can find this at art supply stores or at better camera stores.

Tips for Scanning 3-D Objects

- Scan 3-D objects as a `Black and White` or `Color Photograph`. Most objects will scan better as photographs. For a special effect, you might try scanning a 3-D object as line art (`Black and White Drawing` image type option).

- Experiment with the DeskScan II Highlight and Shadow tool to make the background white so the object will stand out from the background. You may have to remove a bit of gray background with your image editor. You can use your image editor's clipping path (a tool to mask parts of an image) to completely remove the background.

- When scanning 3-D objects, remove the lid from your HP ScanJet color scanner. Place a sheet of clean white paper or a clean white cloth over the object.

- Use the DeskScan II Lasso tool to crop as closely to the object as you can. This will save time when you want to make the background pure white.

- Do not scan anything that is copyrighted or registered. 3-D objects such as cloth, wall paper, or floor tiles can be copyrighted.

Tips for Using Scanned 3-D Objects

You can use scanned 3-D objects just as you would a scanned photograph. You can add background with filters in your image editor. You can add text to the images as Ed did for his barber shop. In fact, anything that you can do with a scanned photograph or drawing, you can do with a scanned 3-D object.

To create the disk label for the fictitious Pretty Flowers, I scanned an actual floppy disk. In Adobe Photoshop, I added the white label area and the text. Next, I rotated the disk and added a shadow with Alien Skin's Eye Candy Shadow filter.

Many enterprising small businesses are using this capability of their HP ScanJet scanner to produce catalogs of jewelry, watches, stamps, coins, badges, buttons, etc. Anything that can safely fit onto the scanner glass is a candidate for this treatment.

How to Add Color to Black-and-White Images

*P*rior to the invention of color photography, artists, designers, and publishers produced color publications and images by printing black-and-white photographs and drawings using colors of ink instead of black ink. Using your image editor and a color printer, you can create the same effects with your scanned images.

Adding Color to Black-and-White Drawings

In Chapter 3, I explained that a black-and-white drawing is a bi-level bitmap, which means that it has only white or black pixels. If the original drawing is already color, you should scan it as a color drawing. But, if you want to add color to a drawing that was originally black-and-white, you can do it with your image editor.

How to Add Color to a Black-and-White Drawing

1. Load a scanned black-and-white drawing into your image editor or use TWAIN to scan directly into the image editor.

2. Change the mode to indexed color.

3. Use the image editor's selection tools to select the parts of the drawing that you wish to change to color. If you wish to change all black to another color, use the editor's magic wand-tool to select the black pixels.

4. Use the fill tool to fill the selected area(s) with the new color.

Use a process color as the fill color if you are planning to use four-color commercial printing for your document. If you are printing only on a desktop color printer, you can use a Pantone color.

Clip art scanned at 600 ppi and saved as a black-and-white drawing image type.

Here I selected some of the black pixels and changed them to green with the fill tool. To see this image in color, refer to Figure 35 in the Color Section.

Duotones, Tritones, and Quadtones

Toning is a process in which a black-and-white photograph is printed using two or more colors of ink. One of the colors is usually black. The other colors are one or more of the process colors used in normal four color CMYK printing (cyan, magenta, or yellow). If you are not doing four-color printing, the color ink can be one of the graphic art inks such as Pantone. Image editors, such as Adobe Photoshop, have duotone capability. You can control the density of the inks to produce the effect you wish. The image editors usually include pre-built combinations that you can use as-is, or you can experiment by changing the density of one or both inks.

How to Create a Duotone

The following example illustrates the process of creating a duotone image from a grayscale photograph. While the example uses Adobe Photoshop, the process is similar with other image editors.

1. Load a grayscale photograph into your image editor or use TWAIN to scan directly into the image editor.

2. Change the mode from grayscale to duotone.

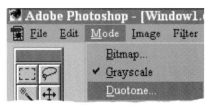

3. Load one of the pre-built options.

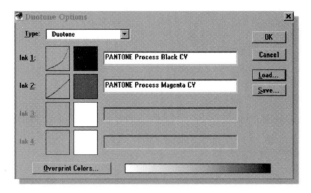

4. If you are satisfied with the effect, click **OK**.

5. If you would like to modify the effect, click on the curve next to the color you would like to modify. Increase or decrease the amount of color. Click on **Save ...** Type a name for your modification and click **OK**.

How to Scan Clip Art

*C*lip art gets its name from the process of clipping or cutting drawings from a book or page of drawings. Today we have electronic clip art already drawn for your use. For many years, artists, illustrators, newspaper and magazine editors used clip art books and they are still available. These are books of drawings that can be purchased in art supply stores or ordered directly from the publisher. Some of the publishers offer a subscription service through which you regularly receive clip art books. Some of these have themes that match the season of the year. There are literally hundreds of clip art books available. Some of the publishers of clip art books have been in the business over one hundred years. Some of these clip art books are actually booklets costing less than five dollars. Some are very large volumes costing over fifty dollars.

There is more clip art available in printed form than in electronic form. This may change in the future as more and more electronic art is produced. Some electronic art is very well done. Some is even drawn by professional illustrators. Some electronic clip art is in the form of scanned bitmapped files that are not any better than you can produce yourself. Better electronic clip art is available in Encapsulated PostScript format that can be scaled without becoming jagged.

Most clip art books that you can purchase for your own publications and documents are copyright-free (some are not, so be sure to check before you scan). Some clip art has restrictions as to how many of the images you may use in one publication. Generally, if you are scanning for personal documents or for limited-run publications such as club or church newsletters, you don't have to be concerned. If you are producing a mass distribution publication such as a magazine or book, you will want to be careful (and lawful) in your use of these clip art images.

Clip art books are available on an amazing variety of subjects and themes. A listing from one producer includes medical and health illustrations, travel and vacation, school and educational subjects, nautical and seashore, sports, wedding illustrations, etc. These books typically include several sizes of the same illustration. In pre-computer days, you would cut out the illustration you needed and tape or paste it onto your camera-ready-art master. If you were not careful, you could destroy the clipping and might have to start again with a new one.

Refer to Page 244 for a list of clip art book publishers.

Scanning clip art offers a number of advantages over clipping or cutting it from a book or page:

- You can use the images more than once.
- You don't have to paste or glue them into your documents.
- You can scan the clip art, trace it with tracing software and convert it to vector art that can be enlarged or reduced without becoming jagged.
- You can use an image editor to create special effects.

Scanned from a Dover clip art book at 600 ppi and saved as a black-and-white drawing.

The same image after conversion to grayscale in Photoshop. Alien Skin Drop Shadow filter was applied to the black pixels.

Do I Scan It as a Drawing or Photograph?

Most clip art consists of black ink on white paper and scans well as a 1-bit `Black-and-White Drawing` with DeskScan II. Some of the newer clip art books contain color images that can be scanned as DeskScan II `Color Drawings`.

Some pieces of clip art are not really black-and-white drawings. Some contain shades of gray and will scan better as `Black-and-White Photographs` (grayscale images) with DeskScan II.

Clip art from a Dover book scanned as a black-and-white drawing at 600 ppi.

Same clip art scanned as a black-and-white photograph at 200 ppi.

Modifying Clip Art

You can modify your scanned clip art with your image editor or if you trace it and convert it to vector format, you can modify it with your drawing or illustration program. You can add filter effects with your image editor and you can add text to the clip art with an image editor or drawing program.

Text added to a scanned image with an image editor becomes part of the bitmapped image and cannot be edited. Some image editors like Photoshop have a layering feature that lets you put the text on a different layer from the scanned image. The text cannot be edited as text, but you can delete that layer and start over again. If you think you might need to change the text, you can import the scanned image into a drawing program and place the text on top of the scanned image. Some drawing programs have a layering feature that also allows you to place the text on a separate layer.

 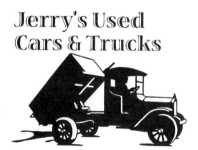

Clip art from a Dover catalog scanned at 600 ppi as a black-and-white drawing.

Text added directly to the scanned image with Adobe Photoshop. This text cannot be edited.

Tracing Scanned Clip Art

If you want to add text that can be edited to clip art, or enlarge an image without it becoming jagged, you can trace the scanned clip art with a tracing program such as Adobe Streamline, or you can use the tracing feature in your drawing or illustration program. Tracing converts the bitmapped image to a vector format consisting of lines and curves that can be edited with a drawing or illustration program such as CorelDRAW or Adobe Illustrator. A benefit of converting the image to a vector graphic is that it will print at the highest resolution of the printer whereas bitmaps will always print at the resolution at which they were scanned.

See Chapter 8 for information on tracing scanned images.

The following examples show the same image scanned as a 600 ppi bitmap and, after tracing, as an EPS file. Both versions are shown enlarged five times.

 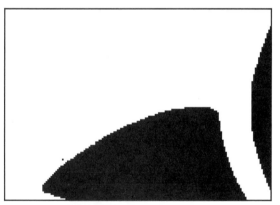

600 ppi TIFF file.   *Same 600 ppi TIFF file enlarged four times.*

 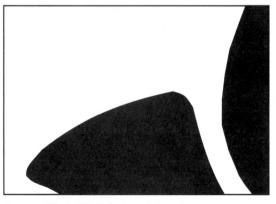

300 ppi EPS file.   *Same 300 ppi EPS file enlarged four times.*

Chapter 10

How to Print
Scanned Images

Introduction

*U*nless you scan exclusively for the World Wide Web or for multimedia, your images will ultimately end up on a piece of paper. Whether you print for limited distribution or your images are used in books and magazines, you will probably print your images first on a desktop black-and-white or color printer.

The introductions of the first laser printer in 1984 and the Adobe PostScript printer language in 1985 made desktop publishing possible. Today, it would be difficult to imagine any office, organization, or home business without a desktop printer of some type. The quality of desktop printers has increased to the point where you can now produce documents on your desktop that can be directly distributed to customers or used as masters for commercial printing. The combination of a desktop printer and your HP ScanJet color scanner makes you a publisher. Someone once said "Freedom of the press belongs to those who own one." You may not own a printing press, but you can have the tools that let you make printing press-quality documents.

This chapter will help you select paper types for printing your scanned images, provide tips on getting the best results with your desktop printer, and show you how to use your desktop printer as a proofing device for commercial four-color printing.

Types of Desktop Printers

*Y*ou almost certainly use some type of black-and-white or color desktop printer to print your scanned images. Unless you work exclusively in multimedia or online Web development, your scanned images will ultimately be printed. Even if your scanned images are destined for a commercial printing press, you will probably proof them on a desktop printer.

Desktop printers have improved tremendously since the early days of dot matrix printers that printed poorly and made a horrible racket that woke up your neighbors and made dogs howl. Today, high-quality desktop printers give excellent color with resolution that is good enough in some cases to use as camera-ready art.

Desktop printers are available in three general categories. There are other types of specialized printers, but the following three types make up the bulk of sales of desktop printers:

- Black-and-white or color inkjet (thermal inkjet)
- Black-and-white or color laser
- Dye sublimation

Black-and-White or Color Inkjet Printers

Most inkjet printers are now color or color-capable. There are not many black-and-white-only models left. Most color printers also print good quality black-and-white images so there is not much need for both types. Inkjet printers are available that range in price from under $200 to over $50,000. The most popular are the line of DeskJet printers from Hewlett-Packard. The high-end models are available from companies such as Iris Graphics.

The Hewlett-Packard DeskJet 1600C is a 300 dpi color printer available with or without Adobe PostScript.

The DeskJet line from HP is intended for general home and office use. Most models do not include PostScript, which is necessary if you plan to use the printer as a proofing device for commercial printing. Some of the DeskJet models offer PostScript as an add-on option. If you plan to use your printer as a proofing device, be sure to look for one with PostScript or one to which you can add PostScript.

The high-end inkjet models, such as the Iris Smartjet line, are intended as final output for some jobs and as high-quality proofing output for others. Because of the inkjet technology they use, they have an apparent resolution of from 1,500 to 1,800 dpi. Some can handle paper as wide as 24 by 24 inches. At prices as high as $50,000 they are obviously not something that many people would have at home or in their small offices. They can normally be found at service bureaus or commercial printers. Some large advertising agencies or large companies that do a lot of publishing may also have them. In most cases, if you need high-resolution inkjet output, you will need to visit a commercial printer or service bureau.

When using a desktop inkjet or even one of the high-quality inkjet printers as a proofing device for commercial printing, keep in mind that they are not 100% accurate as proofing devices. Printing color on paper with ink from an inkjet printer is not the same as printing ink on paper using four-color printing plates on a commercial printing press. The imagesetters used to produce the negatives or paper used to make printing plates produce much smaller dots than do desktop printers. And as they use photographic film or paper, the output is of much higher quality than your desktop printer. It is very important that you work with your commercial printer to review your desktop proofs so that they can point out to you how the final output may differ.

Black-and-White or Color Laser Printers

It was the early Hewlett-Packard LaserJet and Apple LaserWriter black-and-white laser printers that made desktop publishing possible. For the first time, ordinary people had printers that could be used at home or in the office to produce output that was suitable for use as final distribution or as camera-ready art for duplication. The black-and-white laser printer remains the standard for most home use and for small and large offices. Many newsletters, forms, and even small magazines are produced with desktop laser printers. You probably have a laser printer sitting next to your HP ScanJet scanner now.

The new color laser printers have given new capabilities to the small office and home user. You can now create high-quality laser output on your desktop. The current color laser models are not inexpensive. They can cost as much as two or three black-and-white models. They are not particularly fast. The advantage they offer is that they can print on normal office bond paper, if cost of printing is a major factor. As with black-and-white lasers, they are available in both PostScript and PCL models. If you plan to use one as a proofing device for commercial printing, be sure to get the PostScript model or the dual PCL/PostScript option. Be aware that color laser printers do not normally print with the color saturation of an inkjet printer. If you are planning to use laser output for proofing, be sure to consult with your commercial printer.

Dye Sublimation Printers

If you do a lot of proofing for commercial printing, your best choice for a proofing device is probably a dye sublimation printer. This type of printer works by applying heat to a special ribbon containing wax which melts onto the paper. You can get near-photographic quality from a dye sublimation printer. They require special papers and the ink ribbons are far more costly than the ink cartridges of inkjet printers.

The output from a dye sub printer, as they are often called, is so good in most cases that they can be used for final output. This is also their disadvantage! In some cases, the dye sub output looks even better than the four-color output from a commercial printing press. Dye sub printers do extremely well with photographs, but not so well with text and line art such as drawings. Small lines on drawings or small type does not reproduce as well as you would like. These printers produce softer images than imagesetters. This is because a dye sub printer has reduced capability to reproduce sharp edges or rapid tonal transitions. You probably will not rush out to purchase a dye sub printer unless you are a graphic artist or an advertising agency. You can obtain dye sub output from some commercial printers and service bureaus.

Calibrate, Calibrate!

No matter which type of printer you use to output your scanned images, it is most important that it be calibrated for use with your HP ScanJet scanner. The DeskScan II software that accompanies your scanner includes a number of pre-built calibrations for most HP printers. These print path calibrations will get you started quickly, but you should make a custom calibration for your particular printer as soon as possible. Each printer is different and toner and ink cartridges can vary. Take the time to do it! The results will make it worthwhile.

PCL or PostScript?

Your computer must communicate with your printer to print your documents, including your scanned images. The computer software that you use (the operating system and software applications) does not include the capability to communicate directly with printers. Computers communicate with printers with special computer languages. Almost all personal computers (both Macintosh and Windows) use one of two types of printer languages—Adobe's PostScript or Hewlett-Packard's PCL (Printer Control Language). Each is a special type of computer language designed especially for printing (examples of computer languages include Fortran, Basic, Pascal, etc.). You don't have to worry about learning to program in PCL or PostScript (you can if you want to). The PCL and PostScript software takes care of sending documents from your computer to the printer.

Advantages and Disadvantages

PCL and PostScript both have advantages and disadvantages. Whether to use PCL or PostScript will depend on your budget and needs. Following is my take on the advantages and disadvantages of each language:

- Printers equipped with PostScript cost more than ones with PCL.
- If you plan to print your documents on a four-color press (your documents will be color separated), you must use a PostScript printer to proof the documents.
- PCL is built-in on almost all Hewlett-Packard printers. PostScript is sometimes an option.
- PostScript is the standard method of printing on Macintosh computers. PCL does not work with Macs.
- Encapsulated PostScript (EPS/EPSF) files will not print correctly on a non-PostScript printer.

How Much RAM?

*J*ust as computers must have Random-Access-Memory (RAM) to run software programs, printers must also have RAM to print your files. Most desktop printers come with just the minimum amount of RAM to print text-only pages and perhaps some drawings. Most do not come with enough RAM to print full-page scanned images. A typical black-and-white laser printer comes with two megabytes of RAM. This is not enough to print a full-page scanned image. To print a full-page black-and-white scanned image at 600 dpi requires a minimum of four megabytes of RAM. Printers equipped with PostScript will require more RAM than a PCL printer to print the same image (PostScript files are normally larger than PCL files).

Inkjet printers and laser printers use RAM differently. Laser printers must have enough memory (RAM) to receive an entire page before they can start printing. Inkjet printers, on the other hand, only need enough memory (RAM) to print one line of the page.

If you do not know how much RAM you have in your printer, print out the test page (this is sometimes called the configuration page). Look for a statement that says something like this: "Available Printer Memory: 3164" (in kilobytes). Make sure your printer driver software knows how much RAM you have in your printer. This should be detected automatically, but sometimes it isn't. To make sure it is set correctly, go to your printer's **Setup** menu and in the **Properties** dialog, look for a menu item labeled `Device Options`. It will show the amount of available memory in kilobytes. If it is not correct, type in the correct number (it will be on the test printout) and click **OK**. The menus may look different than the example shown here and the text may be slightly different. If you are unsure, consult your printer's documentation or the documentation that accompanied your printer driver software.

Selecting Papers for Desktop Printing

When selecting paper to use on your black-and-white or color desktop printer, look for papers that are as smooth as possible and free of paper dust, lint, or talc. Talc can be found in papers that contain cotton fiber—avoid this type of paper. The talc can flake off the paper and leave a residue in your printer. You may be tempted to use the same paper that you use for your office copy machine—it is already in the supply cabinet! Don't do it! Copy machine papers will not give you the high-quality results that a paper designed for desktop printers produces.

Papers to Look For:

- Brightest white
- Maximum smoothness
- Minimum lint
- Resistance to static

- Moisture-resistant packaging

Papers to Avoid

With laser printers:

- Coated papers
  (The coating may melt and damage your printer.)
- Heavier than 35 pounds
  (Can jam your printer.)

With all desktop printers:

- Lighter than 20 pounds
  (Image may show through to the other side.)
- Foil papers
  (This type of paper can melt and damage your printer.)
- Embossed letterhead paper
  (This type of paper can jam and can also scratch the toner drum in laser printers.)
- Highly textured paper
  (This type of paper will not produce sharp scanned images. Only use this type of paper if you want a special effect.)

Selecting Camera-Ready Papers

You may wish to produce output from your desktop printer that will go directly to a commercial copy center or printing press. In the commercial copy and printing businesses, this is referred to as *camera-ready art*, or CRA, because they often use a graphics art camera to copy your masters for reproduction.

Several paper manufacturers produce camera-ready art papers for use with desktop printers. These papers typically are thicker than normal bond papers used for everyday printing. They are often coated with special materials that make the toner or ink adhere to the papers better than normal papers. Some CRA papers are coated on one side with a special wax. This wax serves to protect the paper from the rubber cement used by paste-up artists. In commercial printing and duplicating facilities, masters are often mounted on special cardboard stock to protect them during the printing and duplicating processes. These mounting boards can be simple white illustration board. Special paste-up boards are also available that have non-reproducing grids for alignment purposes. Some printing and duplicating facilities also protect the front of the masters by spraying them with clear artist's lacquer, or they attach transparent cover sheets to the paste-up boards. Tracing paper is often used as a cover sheet. These pasted-up boards with cover sheets are referred to by printers and artists as *mechanicals*. If you plan to give your duplicator or commercial printer a master copy to print from, you should seriously consider obtaining a stock of camera-ready art paper to use for printing your masters. These papers are considerably more expensive than the normal bond papers used in office printing, but they are worth the cost.

If you do not have access to these special CRA papers, premium-quality gloss papers are available from Hewlett-Packard that can serve as camera-ready papers for many documents.

Printing Scanned Images

*T*o get the best possible prints of your scanned images, your printer must be set up correctly and the various options must be selected carefully to produce the optimum results.

Each printer model and brand will have different options depending on whether it is a black-and-white or color printer and whether it is a PCL or PostScript printer. The Windows and Macintosh operating systems both have software drivers for each printer that have setup and operating options that you should become familiar with. Each one will have defaults that you can use as they come from the manufacturer, but these defaults are not always optimal for printing scanned images and you should learn what each is and what each does. I cannot possibly show every option for every printer, but the following will give you a sample of what to look for. Be sure to consult the documentation for your particular printer and also the documentation that accompanied the printer driver software.

Printer driver software is included with the Windows and Macintosh operating systems and it is also included with the printer. PostScript printer driver software for Windows and Macintosh is also available from Adobe Systems. The advantage of Adobe software is that it includes drivers for imagesetters as well as desktop printers. When you get to the next chapter on high-resolution printing, you will learn why you might want to use the driver for an imagesetter. For now, we will stick to desktop printers.

The following illustration is an example of the `Properties` dialog box for a typical printer (in this case, for a PostScript printer). In this case, you have eight different option dialog boxes for setting the printer's properties or options. The `Properties` dialog box for a different printer will probably have different choices.

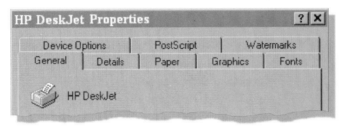

Paper Options

Some printers, such as the Hewlett-Packard DeskJet series, provide options for the type of paper your images will be printed on. You can choose from `Plain Paper` (bond type), `HP Special Paper`, `HP Glossy Paper`, or `HP Transparency` material.

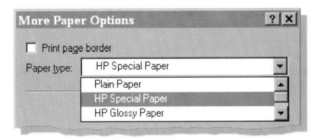

Timeout Values

These options control how long your printer's driver software will wait for data before it gets tired and quits (I am joking). Seriously, your printer is not smart enough to know what you are trying to do. If it does not receive data after waiting a specified amount of time, it will assume that there is something wrong and will time out. It also needs to know how much time to allocate to printing each document or file. When you are printing large files with scanned images, the printer may time out before all of your document or file has been sent to the printer. If you regularly print large files, you should set these values to either 999 (the largest you can enter) or to 0 (zero), which tells the printer to never timeout. There are two options for timeout values:

The first setting (`Job Timeout`) controls how long your printer will allocate to printing each document. If the document is not completely printed within the allocated time, the printer will stop printing that document. Documents that contain scanned images will take longer to print than documents that contain only text. The default value (the one that is built in by the manufacturer is normally too low for printing scanned images. Increase it to 999 or set it to 0 (zero).

The second option (`Wait Timeout`) controls how long your printer will wait for data. If the printer waits longer than the set value, it will stop printing the document. Again, the default value is probably too low; set it to 999 or to 0 (zero).

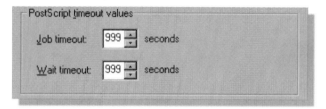

PostScript Header

The PostScript header is a file that contains instructions that must be sent to your PostScript printer. You have the option of sending this file to the printer each time you print (`Download header with each print job`) or you can set up your system to send this file to the printer once when you turn on the printer and computer (`Assume header is downloaded and retained`). If you set it up the second way, you will not have to send the file each time and this will speed up printing. There is also an option button to send the header immediately in case it was not downloaded automatically.

If you typically turn on your printer and leave it on for long periods of time, setting it up to download the header once will save you time each time you print. If you do not leave your printer on for long periods, but turn it on and off frequently, it is probably better to select `Download header with each print job`.

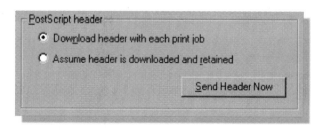

PostScript Options

You will only see these options if you are using a PostScript printer. If your printer does not have PostScript, you may have different options for PCL. The options for PostScript may also be different, depending on the particular printer model. Your options dialog will probably look similar to the example on this page.

Typically, you will have options for the output format. These options will probably read something like the sample shown:

- `PostScript (optimize for speed)`
- `PostScript (optimize for portability)`
- `Encapsulated PostScript (EPS)`

The first option (`optimize for speed`) is used to speed up the printing of large files. The second option (`optimize for portability`) is required by some software programs (Adobe FrameMaker for Windows requires this option when printing to PostScript printers). This option is used to keep any other printer settings from stopping the printing of a document (kind of like a "print no matter what" option). The last option is to be used when you want to print to an Encapsulated PostScript file. You can use this option to print a file that can be sent to someone else and they can print it even if they do not have the software that created it. For example, if you created a document with Adobe PageMaker and you sent an Encapsulated PostScript file of the document to someone who did not have PageMaker, they could print the document on their PostScript printer.

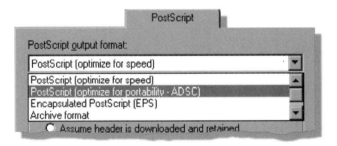

Print Quality

Some printers offer the option to control print quality. You can choose from `Fast` (which gives you the lowest quality), `Normal`, or `High Quality`. Choose `Fast` when you are printing drafts that you want to view as quickly as possible; choose `Normal` for most of your work; and choose `High Quality` when you are ready to produce your final output.

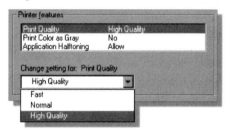

Color Matching

*T*he greatest problem with color printing is trying to get all the pieces of a publishing system (printer, scanner, computer screen, and software) to work together. The goal is to have what you see on the computer screen match what comes out of the printer. This is often a major disappointment to those who are new to color desktop publishing. What they see on the computer screen is darker or lighter than what comes out of the printer…or the colors don't match.

In an attempt to address this problem, a number of companies have developed software to help match the components of a desktop publishing system so that "what you see is what you get" is more than just a slogan. Color management software is available from a number of companies including:

■ Hewlett-Packard ColorSmart

■ Apple ColorSync

■ EFI EfiColor

■ Agfa FotoFlow

■ Kodak Precision CMS

■ Pantone Open Color Environment

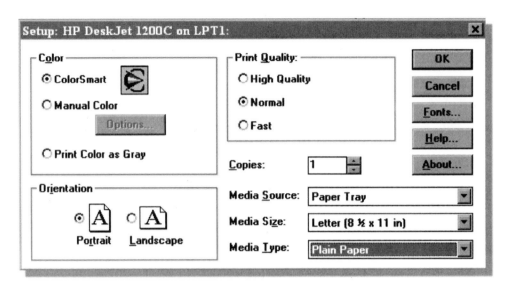

*The setup preferences for the HP DeskJet 1200C includes
HP ColorSmart color matching.*

Some of these, such as EFI EfiColor, are included with software programs
such as QuarkXpress. Apple ColorSync 2.0 is an extension of the Apple
System 7 operating system. Windows 95 includes Kodak's KEPS Precision
CMS color management software and calls it ICM (Integrated Color
Management).

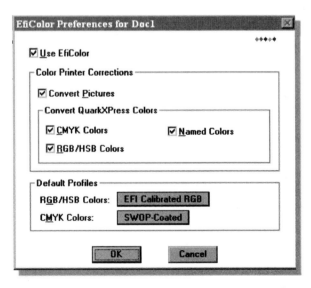

*The EfiColor preferences dialog. EfiColor includes profiles
for a number of devices, and you can create your own.*

Some color matching software only works with certain software applications or certain equipment. For example, HP ColorSmart software does not support PostScript and only works with PCL printers, making it unavailable as a proofing device for most commercial printing. ColorSmart is a good choice for those who do not do commercial printing and who do all of their work with their desktop printer.

Regardless of the color matching system you use, color printing with a desktop printer is often a compromise. You often have to choose between optimizing your printing for text, drawings, or photographs. For example, the Adobe PostScript driver software for the HP DeskJet 1200C/PS gives you the option of optimizing for presentation graphics or photographs. If your document only consists of text or bar charts, this will not be a problem. But if your document contains text, business graphics, and scanned photographs, you have a choice to make.

If you are printing on a non-PostScript HP DeskJet printer using HP's ColorSmart color matching software, your problem is at least partially solved. If you let ColorSmart do the work, it can detect text, graphics, and photographs on each page and set the appropriate color control and halftone options to optimize each.

The color matching options for the HP DeskJet 1200C/PS printer equipped with Adobe PostScript.

Tips for Printing Scanned Images to a Desktop Printer

If you will use the printouts from your desktop printer as your final output, you will want to get the best possible results. The following tips will help you get the optimum output of your scanned images on your desktop printer.

- Set the toner or ink levels of your printer to their minimum levels to produce text and images that are sharp and not too dark.

- Use high-quality paper for your final output. You may wish to have two stocks of paper: one for everyday use and the other for camera-ready art purposes.

- After printing, spray your output with a clear matte artist's lacquer spray to protect the paper and to prevent toner from flaking off or ink from smearing.

Using a Desktop Color Printer as a Proofing Device for Commercial Printing

*I*f you plan to print your documents containing scanned images on a commercial four-color printing press, you may be able to use your desktop color printer as a proofing device. I say "may" because there are sometimes problems with using a desktop printer this way.

Almost all commercial four-color printing is done with Adobe PostScript. For you to be sure that you are obtaining an accurate proof of what the output from a commercial printing press will be, your desktop environment must be as close to the commercial printer's as possible. Use of a non-PostScript printer almost certainly will produce results that are different from what you will get from the printing press. The halftoning methods used by PCL and PostScript printers is different, so your images will probably look different. Color images will certainly look different and your text may have different line endings.

Many desktop color printers either come with PostScript installed or offer it as an option. A printer equipped with PostScript will cost more than a non-PostScript printer. But, if you regularly send files to a commercial printer for four-color printing, you cannot afford to be without a PostScript printer.

Printing Overhead Transparencies

*A*lthough the use of overhead projectors has decreased slightly with the introduction of computer projection systems, many business and professional presentations still involve the use of overhead projectors and overhead transparencies.

Using a black-and-white laser printer or color desktop printer to produce overhead transparencies is a common presentation technique. In addition to text and the typical bar charts produced with a spreadsheet, you can use your HP ScanJet scanner to add drawings and photographs to your presentations.

You do not have to do anything special to the images that you plan to use in your presentations. Scan them as if you were printing to paper using the print path calibration for the particular printer that you will be using to produce the transparencies.

It is very important that you use transparency film designed for your printer. If you use a film that was not designed for your printer, you may damage the printer and you may not get good results. Transparency film designed for use in office copy machines should not be used in your black-and-white laser printer or your desktop color printer. This material can melt and severely damage the components of your printer. In addition, transparency film for copy machines is usually thicker than those designed for desktop printers and your scanned images may have a foggy or misty appearance.

Hewlett-Packard offers premium-quality transparency films for both black-and-white laser printers and for HP DeskJet color printers. They are available from the dealer where you bought the printer. Do not mix these films between printers as each was designed for a particular printer and temperature range.

Chapter 11

How to Print Scanned Images on
a Printing Press

Introduction

Many individuals who started early in desktop publishing and used scanned images quickly discovered that while desktop printers gave much better output than had ever before been possible, they were not capable of producing magazine- and book-quality for many purposes. High-quality magazines and books are typically printed at resolutions of 1250 dpi and higher. Most desktop printers are either 300 dpi or 600 dpi. The few desktop printers that offer 1200 dpi resolution are very expensive and even the quality obtained from plain paper output at such resolutions does not match that obtained from using photographic film or paper in a high-resolution imagesetter.

Many small- and medium-sized publications and company publishing departments turn to commercial printers and service bureaus to produce high-resolution, high-quality output from their desktop publications. These publications often include scanned images.

This chapter will introduce you to the world of service bureaus, commercial printers, high-resolution output, and color separation. This is only an introduction to a very complex process. If you plan to regularly produce high-quality, high-resolution, four-color separated output, you should be prepared for a fairly high learning curve or you should turn to the professionals who do this everyday. If this chapter accomplishes my goal, you will know just how much you (and I) don't know about commercial color printing and it will assist you in selecting good professionals who will (hopefully) help you to produce the outstanding results that your HP ScanJet scanner is capable of.

High-Resolution Output

If you are planning to use your scanned images in a high-quality publication such as a magazine or book, you will probably be using a commercial printing press. Since you want the publication to be high-quality, you will probably want the output to be high-resolution. You can't get high quality by giving the commercial printer a master printed on your 300 or 600 dpi printer. To produce magazine- or book-quality output, the printing process must produce a line screen of at least 133 lpi. A 600 dpi printer produces a line screen of 85 lpi. Your 300 or 600 dpi printer is adequate for proofing purposes, but it is not adequate for high-quality printing. To get high quality, 133 lpi output, you must use a device called an *imagesetter*.

What is an Imagesetter?

An imagesetter is similar to a black-and-white laser printer in that it uses a laser to expose dots onto photographic paper or film. Imagesetters can produce images as high as 5000 dpi. Most types of publications normally use settings of 1200 or 2400 dpi. Imagesetters are expensive devices and require constant care and maintenance. The cost of an imagesetter can range from a low of about $30,000 to over $200,000. Obviously, they are not the type of device you would have around the house to do the church newsletter or even around your small business to do a monthly magazine for a user group. Imagesetters are typically provided by commercial printers or image service bureaus.

Many different models of imagesetters are made by several different companies, including Linotype-Hell, Monotype, and Agfa. The most widely-used imagesetters are the Linotronic line produced by Linotype-Hell Corporation. In 1983, Linotype introduced the Linotronic Model 100 which was the first image-setter to use the Adobe Postscript page description language. Some publishing industry experts have said that the introduction of the Model 100 had as much to do with the development of desktop publishing as the Macintosh, Apple Laserwriter, and PageMaker. For the first time, small publishers could produce typeset documents on a personal computer, proof them on a desktop laser printer, then take the files to a service bureau or commercial printer and have high-resolution output produced from their files.

How Does an Imagesetter Work?

Earlier, I said that imagesetters are similar to desktop laser printers, and they are to an extent! They both use laser technology to expose the output material. Desktop laser printers use normal paper or transparency film. Imagesetters use photographic film or photographic paper to produce their high-resolution output. Imagesetters consist of three components or parts:

- Raster Image Processor (RIP)
- Laser Imager

■ Photographic Processor

In smaller imagesetters, the RIP and imager are probably contained in the same metal cabinet. In larger imagesetters, the RIP and imager are contained in separate metal cabinets. The photo processor is always a separate component and is probably in a separate room (because of the photographic chemicals). The better commercial printers and service bureaus who are concerned about high quality will have separate photo processors for film and paper. I will discuss the differences between using photographic paper and photographic film when I describe imagesetter output.

Raster Image Processor (RIP)

The Raster Image Processor often looks like a tower-style PC and it may be in a room separate from the imagesetter. However, sometimes the RIP is built into the same cabinet as the imagesetter. The purpose of the RIP is to convert the PostScript (it is almost always PostScript) page description files being sent from a PC into a bitmapped image (which in this case is instructions to the imagesetter where to expose each dot on the paper or film). A RIP typically includes a significant amount of RAM and a hard drive so that it can spool the files to the imagesetter. The hard drive may also be used to store typefaces.

Laser Imager

The laser imager is the biggest part of the imagesetter system. This unit is what is commonly shown in photographs or clip art of imagesetters. The larger ones weigh about 400 pounds. The imager is connected to the RIP. The RIP sends images of pages as tiny dots. The laser imager uses mirrors and lenses to expose these dots onto photographic paper or film with a thin laser beam. The imager includes controls that the operator uses to set the resolution (the number of dots per linear inch).

Photographic Processor

Imagesetters expose images onto special photographic film or resin-coated photographic paper. These materials must be developed or processed before they can be used to make printing press plates. Sometimes the photo processor is included with the imagesetter system from the manufacturer. Sometimes the photo processor is purchased separately from another vendor. The important thing for you, the customer, to remember is that the service bureau or commercial printer should use different photo processors for film and paper. In the processing of photographic film and paper, silver is released from the film or paper into the chemicals, which change the chemical makeup of the processing solutions. The processing solutions can be replenished to compensate for these changes, but mixing paper and film processing in the same machine makes it almost impossible to correctly replenish the solutions. A photo processor that is not correctly replenished and calibrated will produce dots that are not the correct size and the film or paper will not have the correct contrast. All of this will affect the quality of the output from the printing press and may result in your images being too light or dark or having poor color quality. If you are attempting to do high-quality publishing, it pays to learn as much as you can about the process of producing camera-ready art and printing plates.

Calibrating Your Scanner for an Imagesetter

To get the best results and to ensure high quality in your high-resolution publications, you must calibrate your HP ScanJet color scanner to match the output device. Optimally, you should calibrate for the actual printing press. Sometimes this may not be possible. You may not have control over the entire printing process or you may not be able to select a commercial printer until after all the images are scanned. If it is not possible to calibrate for the printing press, you should as a minimum, calibrate for the image-setter. To calibrate for an imagesetter, follow the same procedure used to calibrate for a desktop printer. Instead of sending the calibration target directly to the printer, print the target to a file and have the service bureau output the target onto resin-coated paper. Ideally, images sent to an imagesetter should be printed on photographic film, but HP ScanJet color scanners are not set up to scan calibration targets printed on film. When you receive the calibration target on the resin-coated paper, scan the target and create a print path calibration for the imagesetter used. The DeskScan software includes a print path calibration for a Linotronic imagesetter that you can use in an emergency situation, but you should produce your own customized calibration path as soon as possible.

Creating a Print Path Calibration for Commercial Printing

1. Click on **Custom** in the DeskScan II menu.

2. Click on **Print Path** in the **Custom** menu.

3. Click on **New Printer Calibration**.

4. Click on **Create....**

5. Click on **Black and White** or **Color** in the `Printer Information` box. Type the resolution of the imagesetter your printer will be using (if you don't know, ask them!).

6. Click on the **File** button in the Send To box.
   This creates two calibration target files that you can send directly to your commercial printer or import into your software applications to calibrate for them.

7. Select the file type for the black-and-white calibration file. For commercial printing this should be TIFF or EPS. Type a name for the black-and-white calibration file.

8. Click on **Save**.

9. Select the file type for the color calibration file. It should be the same as the black-and-white file. Type a name for the color calibration file.

10. Click on **Save**.

11. Load or import the calibration targets into the software application that you will be using for your commercial printing.

Some word processing and DTP programs use graphic frames to import images (Corel Ventura, QuarkXpress, Adobe FrameMaker, etc.). For the calibration process to work, make the frames for the calibration targets 4 inches wide by 6 inches high. If your software program puts registration marks, crop marks, calibration marks, or any other type of printer markup on the page, turn these marks off before saving the file or printing the target.

12. Place the calibration targets in the exact center (horizontal and vertical) of the pages.

13. Use the software's print command to print the calibration target to a PostScript file (almost all commercial printers and service bureaus use PostScript...check with yours). See Page 224 for instructions on how to create a PostScript file.

14. Take the calibration target files to your commercial printer or service bureau. They will produce a plate-ready negative at the appropriate resolution you have agreed upon. They will then produce printing plates and set up the printing press to produce a short press run.

15. Ask the commercial printer if they can print your targets on different types of paper stock (coated, uncoated, gloss or matte, etc.). The printer will probably not charge you more as long as they do not have to remove the printing plates from the press. When you receive the prints, mark the type of paper used on the backs and save them for future use.

16. Place the black-and-white target carefully on the scanner bed and carefully close the lid.

17. Start the DeskScan II software. Click on **Custom** in the DeskScan II menu bar.

18. Click on **Print Path** in the **Custom** menu.

19. Click on **New** under `Printer Calibration`.

20. Click on **Scan...**

21. Repeat the process for the color target.

22. Type a name for the print path calibration (use the name of the printing company or your project, i.e., `Lino530`)

23. Click on **Done**. The new calibration will now be available for use any time that you scan an image that will be printed with that printer.

Scanning Images for Imagesetters

After you have calibrated your HP ScanJet for the imagesetter and commercial printing press, you should be able to scan as you normally do. An important aspect to keep in mind...high-resolution imagesetters print on photograph film or paper. They do not use the ink or toner as does your desktop printer. In addition to being at a much higher resolution, the images tend to be somewhat lighter. The print path calibration process compensates for that, but this may mean that when you proof your images with your desktop laser or inkjet printer, they may not look perfect to you. Do not be tempted to make them look good on your desktop printer by using the manual controls in DeskScan II or your image editor. A desktop printer is not a perfect proofing device.

Outputting to Film or Paper?

When you send your files to a service bureau for output on a high-resolution imagesetter, you will have the choice of outputting to photographic film or photographic resin-coated paper. You will also have the choice of a positive or negative image. Outputting to a positive image on resin-coated paper gives you the advantage of being able to look at an image that looks very much like your original image. It is positive and printed on paper. The disadvantage is that printing plates must be produced from film. If you have your imagesetter output produced on photographic paper, the printer will have to use a very large, special-purpose graphic arts camera to make a negative of your paper positive. I highly recommend that you have your camera-ready art produced on photographic film (it removes one step in the process and each time an image is copied, something is lost). The service bureau or printer can make a positive proof on paper from the imagesetter negatives.

How Color Is Separated

*T*raditional color separations are made by photographing a photograph or image four times (on separate sheets of film) with special graphic arts cameras using different color filters for each exposure. The result is four negatives that each record different colors. The negatives are exposed through special halftone screens that produce the dots necessary for commercial printing. The screens are rotated at different angles for each exposure so that the dots that are produced do not interfere with each other and produce moiré patterns.

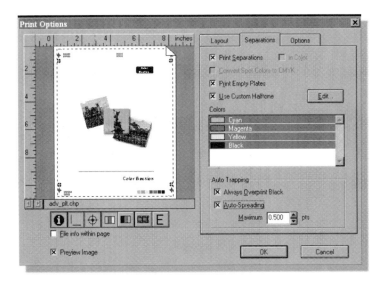

The color separation options in Corel Ventura Publisher 5.0, the program that was used to produce this book. You can use a desktop color printer, such as an HP DeskJet, to quickly determine if you are correctly separating the pages before sending them to a service bureau.

After the negatives are processed, they are used to produce printing plates. Printing plates are normally metal, or possibly plastic. At least four printing plates are required to reproduce a color photograph—one plate each for cyan, magenta, yellow, and black. The printing press passes the paper over each printing plate in turn. Each plate adds its particular color and all four combined produce a full-color image.

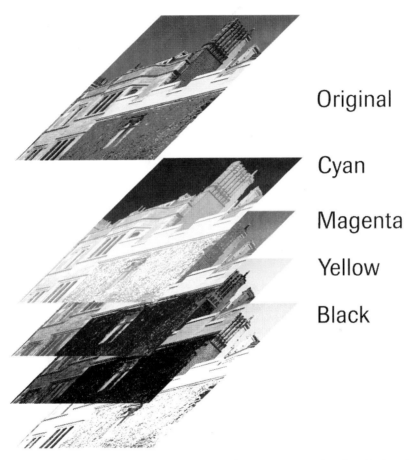

Original

Cyan

Magenta

Yellow

Black

Both traditional and computer color separation produce four black-and-white negatives of the color original. The black-and-white negatives are then used to produce a printing plate for each of the four colors that make up the CMYK printing model.

It is now possible to replace the traditional separation process digitally using special color separation software. Some software programs now include built-in color separation capabilities. Color separation software is also available separately for those applications that do not support color separation. Stand-alone color separation software usually includes more advanced features and capabilities than the built-in versions.

Producing color separations is a skill and not something for the faint of heart or something that can be learned in a few minutes. Software is now available that will give you the capability to produce your own separations, but unless you have had experience working in a service bureau or a commercial printing plant, I recommend you have it done by the professionals.

There are a number of settings and options in color separation software that need to be set after consulting with your service bureau or commercial printer. A quick look at the settings required in Corel Ventura Publisher's separation software, as well as Adobe Separator shown below, shows a bewildering array of settings for halftone, trapping, orientation, emulsion side, etc.

Producing color separations is also complicated by the problems that arise when using a desktop color printer as a proofing device. My advice: Let the pros do it…it will be worth whatever it costs.

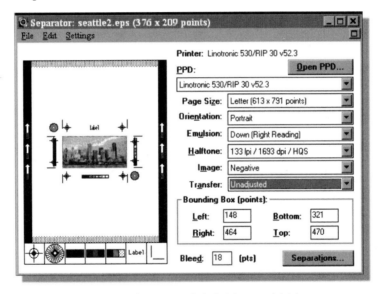

Adobe Separator software is included with several Adobe programs including Adobe Illustrator. This is the initial screen where you choose settings and select options.

Service Bureaus

Service bureaus are a direct result of the DTP revolution that started in the mid-1980's. Those early pioneers needed a way to produce high-resolution output from their new page layout programs. Their 300 dpi desktop laser printers were good enough for some projects and good enough for proofs, but they needed a way to get 1200 or higher dpi output for high-quality publications. The new Adobe PostScript page description language and the introduction of PostScript imagesetters made it possible to proof documents on a desktop printer, then take those same files to a local service bureau where they could get high-resolution output on film or paper.

Some smaller service bureaus only provided imagesetter services. Some commercial printers quickly saw the coming DTP revolution and set up service bureaus as part of their commercial printing operations.

How To Select a Service Bureau

If you live in an urban area, you will probably have a choice of several service bureaus. Sometimes they are listed in the telephone yellow pages as "service bureaus," but often, you will have to look for commercial printers who offer service bureau capabilities. If you live in a rural area or smaller urban area, you may not be able to find a service bureau or commercial printer with service bureau capabilities (not all commercial printers offer electronic publishing or service bureau capabilities). You may be forced to commute to deliver your files, or you may have to resort to shipping your files or transmitting them electronically via modem.

Before giving your files to a service bureau for high-resolution output, there are a number of questions that you should ask:

❏ **Does the service bureau have customers who produce files like yours and use the same software to produce their files?** Be sure to check these references. You don't want to discover that they have had problems after you have given the service bureau your money.

❏ **Does the service bureau use the same version of the application software that you use to prepare the files?**

❏ **Does the service bureau have the same typefaces (fonts) that you use in your files?**

❏ **Does the service bureau have both Apple Macintosh and Microsoft Windows systems connected to the imagesetter?**

Many service bureaus are Mac-only. PostScript and DTP software were first available on the Mac and the first imagesetters only worked with Macs. If the service bureau uses only Macs, it will probably require that you print your Windows files to a PostScript file that the bureau will transfer to the Mac connected to the imagesetter. Most of the time this will not be a problem, but you can encounter problems with typefaces (fonts), and if problems are encountered during the imagesetting process, the service bureau may not have sufficient knowledge of Windows to solve the problem. If you use Windows, it is best to find a service bureau that regularly uses Windows software with its equipment.

❑ **Does the service bureau have tape drives, optical disk drives, Syquest drives, ZIP drives, CD-ROMs, etc. that are compatible with your files?** If your images and files are large, you may not be able to send or take the files on a floppy disk. Before sending tapes or disks, be sure that the service bureau can read them.

❑ **Does the service bureau have file compression and de-compression software that can work with your files?** You may wish to compress the files if you are sending them via modem or if you have limited space on your tapes or disks. Be sure the service bureau can de-compress your files before sending them.

❑ **How does the service bureau charge for its services?** Service bureaus will charge by the page or by the time the imagesetter takes to process your files. Be sure to ask about this before sending your files. Scanned images are often large files and can take a long time to process on an imagesetter. If the service bureau charges by the time required to print your files, your costs could be prohibitive.

❑ **How does the service bureau calibrate its equipment?** Does the service bureau even calibrate it at all? It should calibrate every job with a densitometer (a densitometer is a special type of light meter that measures the density of processed film or photographic paper). Each type of film or paper has standard densities that should be produced when the equipment is working correctly. Quality service bureaus check their equipment almost constantly. Ask to see how your service bureau does it and look for evidence that the bureau is serious about quality. It is difficult for non-professionals to be sure the bureau is quality-conscious. You can look for obvious signs of cleanliness and attention to detail. If the place looks like a pig pen, look for the door!

❑ **Does the service bureau process film and photographic paper in the same processor and chemicals?** It should not! It should use separate photographic processors for film and for paper. When processing photographic films and paper, each produces chemical byproducts (including silver). These byproducts can be removed and/or compensated for by chemical replenishment. The process of replenishment is different for photographic film and paper. Good procedure calls for separate processors for film and paper. Do not let the personnel in a service bureau convince you that it does not make a difference—it does!

❏ **What will the service bureau do if problems are encountered?** Is the service bureau as knowledgeable about your applications as you are? I have actually had to teach service bureaus how to do basic things with my applications (no, I did not use them again). A service bureau that knows what it is doing is worth the money you will pay them.

❏ **Does the service bureau use a replenishment system in their photo processing equipment?** It should! Some use a recirculation system. Replenishment systems add new chemistry as film or paper is processed; a recirculation system stirs up the existing chemicals but does not add any new chemicals.

❏ **Can the service bureau provide paper proofs from their imagesetter negatives?** You should not attempt to make quality assessments from negative images. This is difficult even for professionals to do. You should pay extra to have positive paper prints made.

How to Prepare Files for Service Bureaus

Before sending files to a service bureau, it is vital that you contact the service bureau's customer service department. You will want to ask how to prepare your files for them. Many service bureaus have developed a customer service guide or checklist that outlines the procedures you should follow when sending files to them.

You have two choices of methods when preparing files to be sent to a service bureau:

■ You can send a copy of your application's files (Adobe PageMaker, QuarkXpress, Adobe Photoshop, etc.) to the service bureau. The disadvantage of this method is that if the service bureau has a different version of the application software, you may get unexpected results. Also, the service bureau may not have the same typefaces you used.

■ You can print your application's files to a PostScript file and send this file to the service bureau. The advantage of this method is that you don't have to be concerned if the service bureau has the same version of the application or if they have the same typefaces you used. The disadvantage of this method is that PostScript files can be quite large. Do not attempt to print a PostScript file to a floppy disk. Make sure you have enough free disk space on your hard drive before printing your documents to a PostScript file.

- The PostScript print files you create will almost certainly be too large to fit on a floppy disk. You may be able to compress the files with software. A better solution is to use a tape drive, portable hard drive, CDR writer, optical drive, or a high-capacity removable drive such as an Iomega or Syquest drive (see the previous section on "How to Select a Service Bureau").

- If you regularly use service bureaus to output your scanned images on a high-resolution imagesetter, you should take a look at several special software programs that can analyze your files before you send them to the service bureau and provide information that can help you prepare your files so they will successfully print the first time. FlightCheck from Markzware is a Macintosh program that checks documents created by QuarkXpress, Adobe PageMaker, Adobe Illustrator, and Adobe Photoshop, Macromedia FreeHand, and others for potential imaging problems. There are other such programs for both Macintosh and Windows systems. One of these programs may save you enough money in prepress charges to pay for the program several times over.

How to Create a PostScript Print File in Windows 95

As I stated earlier, you can avoid many problems with service bureaus if you give them Postscript files instead of application files. You avoid font problems and software version differences. To produce a Postscript file that a service bureau can send to its high-resolution imagesetters, you must setup your applications to print to a Postscript file rather than to your desktop printer. The following steps describe the procedure for Windows 95 computers; the procedure for Macintosh systems is different:

1. Install the printer driver software for the imagesetter that your service bureau is using. If it is not on the Windows or Adobe disks, you may be able to obtain a copy from the service bureau. If you cannot obtain the exact driver, you may find one that is similar. Be sure to discuss this with your service bureau before producing the Postscript files.

2. In the Windows 95 **Start** menu, select **Settings**, and then select **Printers**.

3. Click on the icon for the printer you will use to produce your PostScript files (it should be the imagesetter you just installed).

4. Click on **Printer**, and then click on **Properties**.

5. Click on **Details**, and then click on **Add Port**.

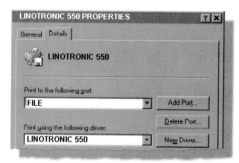

6. When prompted for a port name, type FILE. Close the Properties dialog.

7. From your software application's Print command, click on your printer's name with FILE behind it.

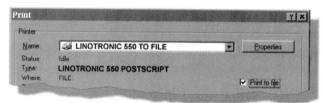

8. From your application's Print command, click on **Print to File**.

9. When prompted, enter a name for your PostScript print file.

Service Bureau Checklist

Producing output on a high-resolution imagesetter in preparation for printing on a commercial printing press is not an inexpensive process. Mistakes can be quite costly. Service bureaus will normally reprint a file free-of-charge if it is their mistake. If you are a regular customer, they might even reprint it if it is your mistake…but don't count on it! Make sure your files are ready before taking them to the service bureau. Print and check, print and check, print and check…as many times as it takes to get it right. Review the following list of do's and don'ts before heading out the door to the service bureau—it just might save you some money.

Do This...

❏ Before preparing your files, talk to the staff at the service bureau or commercial printer. They will surely have suggestions and tips to help you prepare your files. Make sure they understand what you want and what you expect. They will probably have a checklist to help you get ready for high-resolution printing.

❏ Scan your images at the correct resolution for the imagesetter the service bureau will be using for your output. The bureau will tell you what line screen resolution it is using and you can use that to determine your optimal scanning resolution.

❏ If you use a software program such as Adobe PageMaker, make sure you include all linked files. Programs such as PageMaker use PICT or TIFF low-resolution files to display EPS files. If you don't include the linked EPS files, the imagesetter will print the low-resolution (probably 72 ppi) PICT or TIFF files.

❏ Give the service bureau staff a printout of your files. If you have a software program that let you preview imagesetter output on a desktop printer, give them the output from that program. It will help them in their troubleshooting if they encounter any problems.

❏ If you are producing PostScript files for the service bureau, be sure to use the same PostScript drivers it uses. PostScript drivers for most high-resolution imagesetters are available from Adobe Systems in both Macintosh and Windows versions. Sometimes the service bureau can provide a driver that you can use for proofing or printing to PostScript files.

❏ Indicate your preferences on the service bureau's project or order forms. Most forms are in the style of a checklist. See the sample list on the next page.

Don't Do This...

❏ Don't send PICT or BMP files to your service bureau. Service bureaus have had many problems printing these two formats on high-resolution imagesetters. Many service bureaus refuse to accept these two formats. TIFF and EPS are the formats that most service bureaus and commercial printers use and are familiar with and you would be well advised to stick with these two formats.

❏ Don't expect a service bureau to fix your mistakes. Proof and carefully check your files before sending them for high-resolution (and if you aren't careful, high-cost) output.

❏ If you are producing PostScript files for a service bureau, don't put publications with a large number of pages into one file. If there is a problem with one page, the service bureau may not be able to print the rest of the publication.

Service bureaus cannot afford to spend a lot of time trying to figure out why your files will not print. They stay profitable by outputting as many pages per day as they can. If they can't get your file to print, they will probably take it our of their queue and go on to the next job. If you send your project in a number of smaller files rather than one huge one, they can print the parts that work and get back to you on the part that is giving them trouble.

Sample Service Bureau Order Form

Service bureaus or commercial printers almost always have an order form they will ask you to fill out. It will ask a number of questions or will have a number of check boxes for you to use to indicate your preferences. If you do not understand the terminology, ask the staff to explain what each item is and what service or option you are choosing (and how much it costs). The following list is not intended to be all-inclusive, but just a sample of what you might expect to see on an order form.

❏ **Film or Paper?**
Resin-coated paper output is easier to look at and to judge, but printing plates must be made from film. If you opt for paper, the commercial printer will have to shoot negatives of your paper with a graphics camera and this costs more—my recommendation is to always select film.

❏ **Color separations**
You can choose to have the service bureau separate your files, or you can do it yourself—my recommendation is to let them do it!

❏ **Positive or negative?**
Printing plates are made from negatives—so order negatives!

❏ **Emulsion Up or Emulsion Down?**
The emulsion is the side of film that is coated with silver and where the image is recorded. Some printers work with the emulsion side of the film up and some work with it down. Ask your printer about this one!

❏ **Right-Reading?**
This refers also to the emulsion of the film and it means that when you look at the negative produced by the imagesetter with the emulsion side away from you, you will be able to read any text that appears in the negative.

❏ **Orientation** (landscape or portrait)
This indicates whether the page is horizontal (landscape) or vertical (portrait). Imagesetters normally produce film or paper that is wider than most desktop printers. They can rotate a page so that they can get more pages on a sheet of film. They normally place vertical pages horizontally on the imagesetter paper or film. Ask the service bureau to do this—it will save you money!

❏ **Resolution**
Service bureaus and commercial printers typically provide resolutions from 1250 dpi to over 5000 dpi. They probably will charge more for higher resolutions because the files will take longer to print. For black-and-white printing, 1250 dpi is probably adequate. For high-quality black-and-white publications and for four-color printing, higher resolutions should be used. Your service bureau or commercial printer will be able to recommend a resolution based on the type of printing press and the quality of the paper to be used.

❏ **Line screen frequency** (in lines-per-inch)
This also will depend on the type of printing press and the type of paper to be used. Line screen frequency for commercial printing normally starts at about 133 lines-per-inch.

❏ **Screen angle** (in degrees)
For black-and-white printing, there is only one screen angle. For four-color printing, each color has a different angle (to prevent moiré patterns).

Each service bureau or commercial printer will have a different order form with different items. Pay careful attention to these forms—failure to do so could cost you.

Roll the Presses!

*I*t is beyond the scope of this book to describe the commercial printing process. There are numerous types of commercial presses: two-color, four-color, sheet-fed, web, letterpress, offset, gravure, etc. If you wish to learn more about this process, one of the best sources is the excellent set of books and guides published by Agfa Prepress Education Resources (see Chapter 12 for a list). Commercial color printing is a complex and expensive process. It is not the place for the faint-of-heart or the occasional dabbler. It is not the same as printing on your HP LaserJet or HP DeskJet printer. If you plan to print your scanned images on a commercial printing press, your best bet is to find a good service bureau or commercial printing company and get to know them and work with them to get the results your HP ScanJet color scanner is capable of.

Many people are producing excellent publications (newsletters, magazines, books, etc.) using an HP ScanJet color scanner and a commercial printing press. If you are tempted, go for it! Just do it step-by-step and don't be afraid to ask the experts!

Chapter 12

References

Introduction

*O*ne book cannot possibly provide all of the information needed in the fast-changing world of scanning, electronic imaging, and desktop publishing. It is my hope in producing this book to provide the information that will get you started scanning color images for publishing on paper or for the new medium of electronic publishing. The references listed on the following pages provide additional information on scanning, as well as information on several of the software applications described in this book.

I have listed books that I have personally read and that I am familiar with and can recommend. You may obtain these publications by phone, by fax, or by writing to the publisher. I can neither guarantee the availability of these publications nor that the publications listed are the latest editions (new editions are being produced daily).

Several of the periodicals are available free-of-charge to qualified subscribers. Contact the publishers at the addresses listed. It is impossible to assure the availability of publications and the accuracy of addresses shown.

The clip art books contain a variety of images that you may scan and use in your publications. Clip art books may be obtained from art supply stores or directly from the producers listed on Page 244.

Note that some of the publishers of clip art books have restrictions on how many of their images you may use in one publication and some have restrictions on modifications that you may make to the images. Refer to the instructions that accompany each of these books before purchasing them.

Books

Scanning Books

The following books provide additional information on scanning. Most provide information not only on desktop scanners but on high-resolution drum scanners. I provide this list with the acknowledgment that this book you are reading now cannot provide everything that you might want to know about scanning. Several of these books provide a much higher level of detail on such subjects as resolution and halftoning than I provided in this book. If you didn't get enough detail in this book, you may also want to look at one of these.

Super Scanning Techniques
by Jerry B. Day
ISBN 0-679-75157-2
Random House Electronic Publishing
P.O. Box 663
Holmes, PA 19043
(800) 345-8112

Real World Scanning and Halftones
by David Blatner and Steve Roth
ISBN 1-56609-093-8
Peachpit Press
2414 Sixth Street
Berkeley, CA 94710
(800) 283-9444
email: orders@peachpit.com or Web: http://www.peachpit.com

The Windows 95 Scanning Book
by Luisa Simone
ISBN 0-471-11582-7
John Wiley & Sons, Inc.
Professional, Reference and Trade Group
605 Third Avenue
New York, N.Y. 10158-0012

The Verbum Book of Scanned Imagery
by Michael Gosney, Linna Dayton, and Phil Inje Chang
ISBN 1-55851-091-5
M&T Books,
Redwood City, CA 94063
(415) 366-3600

Introduction to Digital Scanning
Agfa Prepress Education Resources
P.O. Box 7917
Mt. Prospect, IL 60056-7917
(800) 395-7007
Fax: (708) 296-4805

The Color Scanner Book
by Stephen Beale and James Cavuto
ISBN: 0-941845-11-7
Micro Publishing Press
2340 Plaza del Amo, Suite 100
Torrance, CA 90501
(310) 212-5802

Start With a Scan
by Janet Ashford and John Odam
ISBN 0-201-88456-9
Peachpit Press
2414 Sixth Street
Berkeley, CA 94710
(800) 283-9444

Color Publishing Books

The following books provide information and instruction on the color printing process, both on desktop color printers and printing with service bureaus and commercial printers on a printing press.

Understanding Desktop Color 2nd Edition
by Michael Kieran
ISBN 1-56609-164-0
Peachpit Press
2414 Sixth Street
Berkley, CA 94710
(800) 283-9444
email: orders@peachpit.com or Web: http://www.peachpit.com

Color Course/Imagesetting (Macintosh only CD-ROM)
ISBN 1-56609-186-1
Peachpit Press
2414 Sixth Street
Berkley, CA 94710
(800) 283-9444
email: orders@peachpit.com or Web: http://www.peachpit.com

Digital Color Prepress
volume 1
Agfa Prepress Education Resources
P.O. Box 7917
Mt. Prospect, IL 60056-7917
(800) 395-7007
Fax: (708) 296-4805

A Guide to Color Separation
Digital Color Prepress volume 2
Agfa Prepress Education Resources
P.O. Box 7917
Mt. Prospect, IL 60056-7917
(800) 395-7007
Fax: (708) 296-4805

Working with Prepress and Printing Suppliers
Digital Color Prepress volume 3
Agfa Prepress Education Resources
P.O. Box 7917
Mt. Prospect, IL 60056-7917
(800) 395-7007
Fax: (708) 296-4805

Color Proofing Guide
Agfa Prepress Education Resources
P.O. Box 7917
Mt. Prospect, IL 60056-7917
(800) 395-7007
Fax: (708) 296-4805

Digital Color Prepress (five volumes of the Agfa Prepress series plus an
interactive CD-ROM)
Agfa Prepress Education Resources
P.O. Box 7917
Mt. Prospect, IL 60056-7917
(800) 395-7007
Fax: (708) 296-4805

Hewlett-Packard's Guide to Color Printing Techniques
by Gordon Padwick
ISBN: 0-679-75323-0
Random House Electronic Publishing
P.O. Box 663
Holmes, PA 19043
(800) 345-8112

Adobe Photoshop Books

The following books provide instruction on how to edit images with Adobe Photoshop. Most cover both Macintosh and Windows versions and some have separate versions for each operating system. Some of the books include CD-ROMS with sample files, sample filters, etc.

Macworld Photoshop 3 Bible
by Deke McClelland
ISBN 1-56884-15B-2
IDG Books Worldwide, Inc.,
919 E. Hillsdale Blvd., Suite 400
Foster City, CA 94404
(415) 655-3000

Photoshop 3 for Windows 95 Bible
by Deke McClelland
ISBN: 1-56884-882-X
IDG Books Worldwide, Inc.
919 E. Hillsdale Blvd., Suite 400
Foster City, CA 94404
(415) 655-3000

The Photoshop Wow 3 Book
by Linnea Dayton and Jack Davis
ISBN 1-56609-178-0 (Macintosh version)
ISBN 0-201-88370-8 (Windows version)
Peachpit Press
2414 Sixth Street
Berkeley, CA 94710
(800) 283-9444
email: orders@peachpit.com or Web: http://www.peachpit.com

Visual Quickstart Guide; Photoshop for Windows
by Elaine Weinmann and Peter Lourekas
ISBN 0-201-88665-0 (Macintosh version)
ISBN 0-201-88625-1 (Windows version)
Peachpit Press
2414 Sixth Street
Berkeley, CA 94710
(800) 283-9444
email: orders@peachpit.com or Web: http://www.peachpit.com

Designer Photoshop
by Rob Day
Random House Electronic Publishing
400 Hahn Road
Westminster, MD 21157
(800) 733-3000

Adobe Photoshop 3 Classroom in a Book
ISBN: 1-568830-118-9 (Macintosh version)
ISBN: 1-568300-120-0 (Windows version)
Adobe Press, Hayden Books
201 West 103rd Street
Indianapolis, IN 46290
(800) 428-5331

Advanced Adobe Photoshop 3 Classroom in a Book
ISBN: 1-56830-116-2 (Windows version)
ISBN: 1-56830-117-0(Macintosh version)
Adobe Press, Hayden Books
201 West 103rd Street
Indianapolis, IN 46290
(800) 428-5331

Photoshop In Black and White, 2nd Edition
by Jim Rich and Sandy Bozek
ISBN: 1-56609-189-6
Peachpit Press
2414 Sixth Street
 Berkeley, CA 94710
(800) 283-9444
email: orders@peachpit.com or Web: http://www.peachpit.com

Inside Adobe Photoshop
by Gary David Bouton and Barbara Mancusio Buton
ISBN: 1-56205-662-X
New Riders Publishing
201 West 103rd Street
Indianapolis, IN 46290
(317) 581-3500

Adobe Photoshop 3 Filters and Effects
by Gary David Bouton and and Gary Kubicek
ISBN: 1-56205-448-1
New Riders Publishing
201 West 103rd Street
Indianapolis, IN 46290
(317) 581-3500

Photoshop 3 Special Effects How-To
by Sherry London
ISBN: 1-878739-76-X
Waite Group Press
200 Tamal Plaza
Corte Mandera, CA 94925
(800) 368-9369
Web: http://www.waite.com/waite

Adobe Photoshop Complete
by Jim Rich
ISBN: 1-56830-323-8
New Riders Publishing
201 West 103rd Street
Indianapolis, IN 46290
(317) 581-3500

Real World Photoshop 3
by David Blatner
ISBN: 1-56609-169-1
Peachpit Press
2414 Sixth Street
Berkeley, CA 94710
(800) 283-9444
email: orders@peachpit.com or Web: http://www.peachpit.com

Fundamental Photoshop, Second Edition
by Adele Droblas Greenberg and Seth Greenberg
ISBN: 0-07-882093-6
Osborne McGraw-Hill
2600 Tenth Street
Berkeley, CA 94710
(800) 822-8158
email: 7007,1531@compuserve.com

Photoshop in 4 Colors, Second Edition
by Mattias Nyman
ISBN: 0-201-88424-0
Peachpit Press
2414 Sixth Street
Berkeley, CA 94710
(800) 283-9444
email: orders@peachpit.com or Web: http://www.peachpit.com

Plug-In Power
by Stephen Beale
ISBN: 0-941845-15-fl
Micro Publishing Press
2340 Plaza del Amo, Suite 100
Torrance, CA 90501
(310) 212-5802

KAI'S Power Tips & Tricks CD-ROM
(Macintosh and Windows versions combined)
MetaTools Inc.
6303 Carpinteria Avenue
Carpinteria, CA 93013
(805) 566-6200
email: America Online: KPTSUPPORT,
Internet: kptsupport@aol.com, or Web: http://www.metatools.com

Photoshop 3: Training on CD (Macintosh-only CD-ROM)
by Quay2 Multimedia
ISBN: 0-201-88409-7
Peachpit Press
2414 Sixth Street
Berkeley, CA 94710
(800) 283-9444
email: orders@peachpit.com or Web: http://www.peachpit.com

Macworld Photoshop Tech Support
by Dawn Erdos
ISBN: 0-7645-4000-9
IDG Books Worldwide, Inc.
919 E. Hillsdale Blvd., Suite : 400
Foster City, CA : 94404
(415) 655-3000

Photoshop 3 for Macs
 ISBN: 1-56884-208-2
 IDG Books Worldwide, Inc.
919 E. Hillsdale Blvd., Suite : 400
Foster City, CA : 94404
(415) 655-3000

Photoshop 3 for Macs for Dummies Quick Reference
ISBN: 1-56884-968-0
IDG Books Worldwide, Inc.
919 E. Hillsdale Blvd., Suite : 400
Foster City, CA : 94404
(415) 655-3000

Photoshop Web Magic
by Renee LeWinter and Ted Schuman
ISBN: 1-56830-314-9
New Riders Publishing
201 West 103rd Street
Indianapolis, IN 46290
(317) 581-3500

Adobe Photoshop Creative Techniques
by Denise Selks, Ellenn Beharian, and Gary Payssick
ISBN: 1-56830-132-4
New Riders Publishing
201 West 103rd Street
Indianapolis, IN 46290
(317) 581-3500

Corel PHOTO-PAINT Books

To my knowledge, these are the only books that have been written on Corel PHOTO-PAINT, but they are probably the only ones you will need. The author is the recognized expert on Corel PHOTO-PAINT (he wrote the user guides for Corel). David also writes regularly on PHOTO-PAINT for *Corel Magazine.*

Corel PHOTO-PAINT Unleashed
by David Huss
ISBN 0-672-305-30516-X
Sams Publishing
201 West 103rd Street
Indianapolis, Indiana 46290
(800) 835-3202
Web: http://www.mcp.com

The Official Guide to Photo-Paint 6
by David Huss
ISBN 0-07-882207-6
Sams Publishing
201 West 103rd Street
Indianapolis, Indiana 46290
(800) 835-3202
Web: http://www.mcp.com

Corel Photo-Paint 7
The Official Guide
by David Huss
ISBN 0-07-882321-8
Sams Publishing
201 West 103rd Street
Indianapolis, Indiana 46290
(800) 835-3202
Web: http://www.mcp.com

Adobe PhotoDeluxe Books

PhotoDeluxe is a new entry in the image editor arena. It is meant to be easier to use than previous image editing software.

Photo Magic with PhotoDeluxe
by Daniel Grotta and Sally Grotta
ISBN: 1-56884-883-8
 IDG Books Worldwide, Inc.
919 E. Hillsdale Blvd., Suite : 400
Foster City, CA : 94404
(415) 655-3000

The Amazing PhotoDeluxe Books for Windows
by Kate O'Day and Linda Tapscott
ISBN: 1-56830-286-X
New Riders Publishing
201 West 103rd Street
Indianapolis, IN 46290
(317) 581-3500

Periodicals

Adobe Magazine
411 First Avenue S.
Seattle, WA 98104
(206) 622-5500

Before & After
1830 Sierra Gardens Drive,
Suite 30
Roseville, CA 95661
(916) 784-3880

Color Publishing
P.O. Box 3184
Tulsa, OK 74101
(508) 392-2157

Computer Artist
P.O. Box 3188
Tulsa, OK 74101-9632
(918) 831-9405

Computer Graphics World
P.O. Box 21638
Tulsa, OK 74121-9980
(918) 835-3161 ext. 400

Corel Magazine
Ariel Communications, Inc.
P.O. Box 202380
Austin, TX 78720-9888
(512) 250-1700

Create Magazine
751 Laurel Street, #335
San Carlos, CA 94070
(608) 278-0700

Design Graphics
Mail America
2323 Randolph Avenue
Avenel, NJ 07001
(800) 688-6247

Digital Imaging
2340 Plaza Del Amo, Suite 100
Torrance ,CA 90501-9959
(310) 212-5802

Dynamic Graphics
Dynamic Graphics, Inc.
6000 N. Forrest Park Dr.,
Peoria, IL 61614-3592
(800) 255-8800

PC Graphics & Video
P.O. Box 5374
Pittsfield, MA 01203-9399
(800) 854-3112

The Page
661 Roscoe Street
Chicago, IL 60657-2926

Photo Electronic Imaging
57 Forsyth St. NW, Suite 1600
Atlanta, GA 30303
(404) 522-8600

Publish
Subscriber Services
P.O. Box 55400
Boulder, CO 80322
(800) 274-5116

Photoshop Techniques
c/o Swanson Tech Support
P.O. Box 30049
Seattle, WA 98103
(206) 682-4315

Step-By-Step Electronic Design
Dynamic Graphics, Inc.
6000 N. Forrest Park Dr.,
Peoria, IL 61614-3592
(309) 688-2300

Clip Art Sources

ARTmaster
500 N. Claremont Blvd.
Claremont, CA 91711
(714) 626-8065

Dover Publications
31 East 2nd Street
Mineola, NY 11501
(516) 294-7000

Dynamic Graphics, Inc.
60000 North Forest Park Dr.
P.O. Box 1901
Peoria, IL 61666-1901
(800) 255-8800

Scanned from a Dover Publications clip art book as a black-and-white drawing at 600 ppi.

Graphic Products Corporation
Rolling Meadows, IL 60008

Dick Sutphen Studio
P.O. Box 38
Malibu, CA 90265
(818) 889-1575

The Church Art Works
875 High Street, N.E.
Salem, OR 97301
(503) 370-9377

Volk Clip Art
P.O. Box 347
Washington, IL 61571-0347
(800) 227-7048

Scanned from a Dynamic Graphics clip art book as a black-and-white photograph at 200 ppi.

Photoshop-Compatible Plug-in Filters

*F*ollowing are special-effects filters that support the Adobe Photoshop plug-in format. These filters can be used with Adobe Photoshop, Corel PHOTO-PAINT 6.0, Macromedia Xres 2.0, Fractal Design's Painter, MicroFrontier's Color It, Pixel Resource's PixelPaint Pro3, Deneba Software's Canvas, Adobe Premiere, Ray Dream Designer, and any other program that supports the Photoshop plug-in format.

Andromeda Series 1 *through* 4 (Macintosh and Windows versions)
Andromeda Software Inc.
699 Hampshire Road, Suite 109
Thousand Oaks, CA 91361
(800) 547-0055

Eye Candy 3.0 (Macintosh and Windows versions)
Alien Skin Software
800 Saint Mary's Street
Raleigh, NC 27607
(919) 832-4124
CompuServe: 72773,777
America Online: Alien Ops or Alien Skin
Internet: alien@vnet.net, or Web: http://www.alienskin.com/alienskin

Kai's Power Tools 3.0 (Macintosh and Windows versions)
MetaTools Inc.
6303 Carpinteria Avenue
Carpinteria, CA 93013
(805) 566-6200
America Online: KPTSUPPORT,
Internet: kptsupport@aol.com, Web: http://www.metatools.com, or
CompuServe: 71333,3542

KPT Convolver 1.0 (Macintosh and Windows versions)
MetaTools Inc.
6303 Carpinteria Avenue
Carpinteria, CA 93013
(805) 566-6200
America Online: KPTSUPPORT,
Internet: kptsupport@aol.com, Web: http://www.metatools.com, or
CompuServe: 71333,3542

Adobe Gallery Effects (Volumes *1, 2,* and *3*)
(Macintosh and Windows versions, also included with Photoshop 4.0)
Adobe Corporation
411 First Avenue South
Suite 200
Seattle, WA 98104-2871
(800) 685-3537

Typo Graphic Edges
(Macintosh version only)
Auto F/X
189 Water Street Box 112
Exeter, NH 03833
(800) 839-2008

Photo/Graphic Edges (Volumes *1, 2,* and *3*)
(Macintosh and Windows versions)
Auto F/X
189 Water Street Box 112
Exeter, NH 03833
(800) 839-2008

Paint Alchemy 2.0
Xaos Tools
600 Townsend Street, Suite 270 East
San Francisco, CA 94103
(800) 289-9267

TypeCaster
(Macintosh version only)
Xaos Tools
600 Townsend Street, Suite 270 East
San Francisco, CA 94103
(800) 289-9267

CyberMesh 1.11
Knoll Software

Pattern Workshop
MicroFrontier
P.O. Box 71190
Des Moines, IA 50322
(515) 270-8109
(800) 388-8109
Internet: MFrontier@aol.com

TextureScape
Specular International
479 West Street
Amherst. MA 01002
(800) 433-7732
Internet: specular@applelink.apple.com, or
Web: http://www .specular.com

Phototools 1.0 *and Intellihance* (Macintosh and Windows versions)
Extensis
55 WE Yamhill Street, Fourth Floor
Portland, OR 97204
(800) 796-9798
http://www.extensis.com

Shareware Plug-in Filters

The following Photoshop plug-in filters are available as shareware or freeware, meaning they are available for a small fee or for free. They are available in most cases only online on the Internet or from a commercial service such as American Online or CompuServe.

Bump 1.0
AtoZ Software
atozsoft@aol.com

Lumpy Noise
Paul Badger
pbadger@cgrg.ohio-state.edu

Sucking Fish 1.01
Naoto Arakawa
gca00443@niftyserve.or.jp

PhotoMagic 2.0.1
DayStar Digital
(770) 967-2077
http://www.daystar.com

Kwick Mask, Create B/W, and *Rotate Color*
Hugh Kawahara
http://www.stanford.edu/-kawahara

Chris Filters
Chris Cox
cc4@andrew.cmu.edu

PhotoNavigator
Xtensis
(503) 274-2020
http://www.extensis.com

Colophon

*T*his book was produced with Intel 486 and Pentium-based computers running Microsoft Windows 95. Body text was typeset with Adobe Minion and Minion Expert typefaces. Chapter and section headings were set with Adobe Tekton and page headers with Adobe Imago Book. Microsoft Word 97 was used for text preparation and the pages were formatted with Corel Ventura Publisher 5.0. All images were scanned with a Hewlett-Packard ScanJet 3c scanner and HP DeskScan II version 2.4 software. Some scanned images were edited or modified with Adobe Photoshop 4.0 or Corel PHOTO-PAINT 6.0. Special effects were added to some images with plug-in filters, including: Kai's Power Tools 3.0, KPT Convolver 1.0, Andromeda Series 2 filters, Alien Skin Software's Eye Candy, AutoF/X Photo/Graphic Edges, and Adobe Gallery Effects. Traced images were produced with Adobe Streamline 3.0 or Corel TRACE 6.0. Adobe Illustrator 4.1 and CorelDRAW 6.0 were used to edit traced images. Illustrations of computer screens were captured with Quarterdeck's Hijaak PRO. Page proofs were produced with a Hewlett-Packard LaserJet 4MP laser printer or a Hewlett-Packard DeskJet 1200C/PS color printer. The color section of this book was printed by Holly Press. The black and white portion was printed by Courier Westford Inc.

All photographs, unless otherwise noted, were produced by the author.

The icon aides were designed and produced by Paul Cackowski of Twin Rivers Design in Johnstown, Colorado.

Glossary

I have included in this glossary words and terms that are used in this book as well as words and terms from the photography and publishing fields that I felt would help you to understand scanning.

additive primary colors   Red, green, and blue are the primary colors of light that when combined produce white light. They are the basis of human vision, color photography, and color television. Your HP ScanJet color scanner produces images that are made of measurements of red, green, and blue light. See subtractive primary colors and CMYK.

application   Computer software that performs specific tasks such as word processing, image editing, scanning, etc. The other major type of computer software is an operating system such as Windows 95, Mac System 7, UNIX, etc. that performs general tasks such as file saving, printing, etc.

Automatic Document Feeder (ADF)   An optional accessory for your HP ScanJet color scanner that automatically feeds in stacks of paper for use with Optical Character Recognition software.

automatic exposure   The DeskScan II software automatic feature that analyzes then optimally sets the contrast and brightness values for the best image quality.

automatic find   The DeskScan II software automatic feature that creates a selection area to just fit your original and performs an analysis on this selected area.

auto trace   A feature of tracing programs and illustration programs that automatically traces bitmapped images and creates vector graphics.

bit   Abbreviation of *binary digit.* The numerical basis for digital information and images. A bit can have a value of either zero or one.

bit depth   The amount of color or tones in an image as determined by the number of bits used to represent the number of possible tones, or shades, that each pixel might take on.

bitmap   The arrangement of picture elements (pixels) in a grid. Each pixel is defined by a set of bits. The number (or numeric value) stored in the pixel defines its shade or tone. In a 1-bit image, each white pixel is a 0 and each black pixel is a 1. In multi-bitmap images, shades of gray or colors are defined by other values stored in each pixel.

brightness   The overall intensity of an image expressed as a numerical value.

byte   The measurement of file size. One byte holds eight bits.

CAD   Abbreviation of *Computer-Aided Design*. A special type of illustration or drawing software used by engineers, designers, and drafting personnel. Previously, CAD software was only found on UNIX computer workstations, but it is now available on Windows and Macintosh systems.

calibration   A software and hardware procedure that sets your HP ScanJet scanner and DeskScan II software to compensate for changes that software application programs and printers make to scanned images. Calibration ensures accurate and consistent results.

Camera-Ready Art (CRA)   A printing industry term that describes the finished version of a publication. In pre-computer publishing days, finished pages were photographed with a large graphic arts camera and the resulting negatives were used to produce printing plates. Today, electronic files can be sent directly to a high-resolution imagesetter and can bypass the camera state, but the term CRA is still used to describe the final version of a document.

CCD   Abbreviation of *Charge Coupled Device*. The part of the HP ScanJet scanner that measures the light reflecting from the original photograph, drawing, or document.

CD-ROM   Abbreviation for *Compact Disc-Read-Only Memory*. A 5-¼ inch disc, similar to music CDs, that stores large amounts of data. Some discs can store up to 650 megabytes of data.

color separation   The process of separating one RGB (Red, Green, and Blue) image into separate Cyan, Magenta, Yellow, and Black (CMYK) images that are used to produce negatives that are in turn used to produce CMYK printing plates used on commercial four-color printing presses.

compression   A software process that reduces the sizes of files including scanned images. TIFF and PICT files can be compressed by the HP DeskScan II software.

contrast   The range of tones or colors in an image. Contrast is a measurement of the difference between the lightest and darkest parts of an image.

cropping   Selecting a portion of an image and discarding the remainder.

density   A measurement of the lightness or darkness of all or part of an image.

densito-   A special type of light meter used by photographic and graphic arts
meter   professionals to measure the density of negatives or photographic
                     prints. It measures the light that is transmitted by a negative or reflected
                     by a print. It is used to measure the negatives and special photographic
                     papers used to produce printing plates in commercial printing and to
                     compare against standard, expected values.

dialog box   The visible window in a software program that prompts you to enter
                     information or select options.

diffusion   One of the HP DeskScan halftone types. It simulates grayscale by
                     distributing the dots in an image in a random pattern.

dithering   A method of grouping precisely calculated, but apparently same-size
                     dots to represent larger dots of different sizes. Conventional halftoning
                     uses dots of different sizes to represent shades of gray. Larger dots
                     represent black areas and smaller dots represent lighter grays or white.
                     Dithering groups same-size dots close together to simulate a larger dot.

dot gain   A percentage measurement of the amount that ink spreads when ap-
                     plied to a paper surface. Dot gain is greater with matte surface paper
                     and less with glossy paper. Dot gain makes images darker and must be
                     compensated for when using commercial printing presses.

dpi   An abbreviation of *dots-per-inch*. A measurement of the resolution of
                     desktop and high-resolution printers in dots per-linear-inch.

drawing   An image made up of vectors (lines and curves).

draw   Computer software that creates graphics using lines and curves rather
program   than bitmaps. Examples of draw programs include CorelDRAW, Adobe
                     Illustrator, and Macromedia FreeHand.

driver   A small software program that is used by the operating system and
                     application software to format data and transfer it to and from periph-
                     erals such as scanners and printers.

DTP   Abbreviation for the term *desktop publishing*. The process of using
                     personal computers and special software to produce publications such
                     as magazines, newsletters, and books. Desktop publishing is used to
                     describe both the process and the software used in the process. Paul

Brainard, founder of Aldus Corporation, first used the term in 1985 to describe his new PageMaker program.

dynamic range   The gradations from light (highlights) to dark (shadows) in an image. A range of densities. Usually refers to the range from the lightest light to the darkest dark supported by photographic film, photographic paper, a scanner, etc.

Encapsulated PostScript (EPS/EPSF)   A graphic file format. EPS was developed primarily for vector graphics but can also be used to store bitmapped images. EPS is special form of Adobe PostScript. When used on Windows computers it is known as "EPS" and with Macintosh as "EPSF." You can only print EPS files on a PostScript printer.

file format   The way in which data such as a scanned image is stored. Examples of file formats include TIFF, PCX, EPS, JPEG, etc. A file usually includes a header that describes the image data and also the image bitmap itself.

FPO   Abbreviation for *For Position Only*. A term used to describe the process in which photographs or drawings are temporarily placed on a page to determine exact location and placement. In pre-computer days, the photographs or drawings would be taped or glued in place. With scanners, a low-resolution image may be used temporarily until the final layout is determined, then it will be replaced by a scan with the final resolution.

grayscale   The measure of grayness of any area of a picture. Grayscale is one of the image types supported by the HP DeskScan II software. When a picture is scanned, the gray level of each pixel of the image is determined and sent to the computer. Dithered images or halftones are not grayscale; they are a type of line art that creates an impression of gray.

halftone   The process of simulating grays and colors using black or colored dots of various sizes. Halftoning is necessary because laser printers, desktop color printers, and commercial printing presses cannot print with gray ink.

halftone dot   Different-sized black or colored shapes created by turning on and off particular spots during printing—on a laser printer, or imagesetter, or on a printing press. Halftone dots are shapes that repeat at a regular angle. This repeating pattern produces the illusion of continuous tone. Halftone dots are not the same as printer dots.

highlight   The lightest part of an image. A cloud in the sky might be an example of a highlight.

HSV   Abbreviation for *Hue, Saturation, and Value.* HSV is a color space model used by computer graphic software programs because of its easy manipulation by image processing algorithms.

imagesetter   A special type of printer that prints on photographic film or paper to produce high-resolution text and graphics. Most imagesetters use the Adobe PostScript printer language.

image type   The way an image will be scanned and/or reproduced. The image types available in DeskScan II software are black-and-white and color drawings (or line art), black-and-white and color halftones, and black-and-white and color photos.

inkjet   A desktop printer that prints by spraying black or color ink on paper.
printer   Inkjet printers can print in varying resolutions.

inverting   A feature in HP DeskScan software that lets you change a positive image to a negative image, or vice versa. HP DeskScan cannot convert a color negative scan into a positive image.

jaggies   A term used to describe the jagged edges that are sometimes seen on bitmapped images that are enlarged too much or that are rotated; especially seen in line art.

JPEG   Abbreviation of *Joint Photographers Experts Group*, the organization that developed the file format. JPEG is a graphics file format that includes "lossy" file compression. When used with Windows computers, JPEG files have the file extension .JPG.

line art   Drawings or graphics that consist of black-and-white only—no shades of gray.

line screen   A measure of the distance between centers of halftone dots as they repeat along the screen angle (also known as screen ruling). The number of halftone dots that can be in an inch and measured in lpi (lines-per-inch).

live   A DeskScan II software feature that automatically redisplays the image
preview   shown in the Preview area when changes are made to scanner settings.

masking   An feature of image editing and illustration software that uses opaque images to block (mask) parts of an image.

matrix   The square grid that forms each halftone dot.

megabyte   Measurement of computer files and disk space. A one-megabyte file has 1,048,576 bytes, or 1,024 kilobytes.

midtones   The part of a grayscale or color image between the highlights and shadows.

moiré   An interference pattern that is produced when an image that has been halftoned (such as a photo in a magazine) is scanned and printed. The halftone pattern that is produced when the image is printed overlaps with the pattern that was already in the image. Moiré patterns can appear as a checkerboard pattern, dots, or wavy lines.

offset printing A process used in commercial printing. A photographic negative is used to produce a metal or plastic printing plate. This plate is then attached to a revolving cylinder. Black or color ink is then applied to the plate and transferred to a rubber blanket attached to another cylinder. The paper is passed over this blanket where it is transferred (or offset) to the paper.

OCR   An abbreviation of *Optical Character Recognition*. The method used to scan text and convert the scanned image to text that can be edited with a text editor or word processor.

paint program A computer graphics program that creates bitmapped images and can also modify and edit scanned images. Also called image editors. Examples include Adobe Photoshop and Corel PHOTO-PAINT.

PCL   An abbreviation of *Printer Control Language*. A computer language developed by Hewlett-Packard for printing text and graphics on desktop printers.

PCX   An abbreviation for *PC Paintbrush Extension*. A graphics file format originally developed by Zsoft Corporation. The PCX format was one of the first graphic file formats for MS-DOS computers.

PICT   Abbreviation of *PICTure*. An image file format that can be either a bitmap or a vector graphic. This format was developed for the original Macintosh computer in 1984.

pixel   Abbreviation of *picture element.* Sometimes called a *pel.* Pixels are square dots that make up scanned images. Each pixel is assigned some number of binary digits (called bits) that define its shade of gray or color.

posteriza-tion   An effect that results when an image has a limited number of shades of gray or colors. This effect can be created deliberately or accidentally by scanning an image with an inappropriate image type selected. Posterization happens when insufficient pixel depth is used to capture all of the colors or shades of gray that were in the original.

PostScript   A page description language that is used to print text and graphics. A printer must be equipped to interpret and print PostScript. PostScript is the de facto standard in the professional publishing and printing industry. PostScript was developed by Adobe Systems in 1984 for the first Apple Laserwriter printer.

PNG   Abbreviation of *Portable Network Graphics.* A new graphic file format developed by the PNG Working Group and sponsored by the World Wide Web Consortium to overcome the legal difficulties with and technical limitations of the GIF file format.

ppi   Abbreviation of *pixels-per-inch.* A measurement used to express or quantify resolution in scanners. It is the measure of the number of pixels (picture elements) per linear inch in a scanned image. A 300 ppi scanner produces 90,000 pixels per square inch. Many computer publications use dots-per-inch (dpi) when describing scanners, but ppi is a more accurate term. In this book, I use ppi when describing scanners and dpi when describing printers.

preview scan A quick scan of the object on the scanner glass often at less than the resolution of the computer screen. The preview scan allows the user to select parts of the image, to make exposure, contrast, and brightness adjustments, and to select other DeskScan II options. After all options are selected, a *final scan* is performed.

raster graphic Also known as a bitmapped graphic. Takes its name from the rasterization of the computer or television screen. It is a graphic image consisting of a dot-by-dot representation of the original.

resolution   To the human eye, it is the amount of detail in a graphical image. Technically, it is a measurement of the number of pixels-per-inch in a bitmapped image or the number of dots-per-inch in a printed image or document. Generally, the higher the resolution, the more detail is visible in an image. It is important to match the resolution of the scanned image to the printer being used. The image cannot be printed at a higher resolution than that of the printer. If the image resolution is higher than needed, you have wasted file space and the image does not look any better. Resolution is a measure of how much detail can be *resolved* by that rate of image sampling.

resin coated (RC) A special type of rapid-drying photographic paper that is used in the printing industry for producing camera-ready art masters with high-resolution imagesetters.

RGB Abbreviation for *Red-Green-Blue*. A color model used by computer monitors to display color images and by color scanners such as the HP ScanJet.

screen The method used in commercial printing to produce a halftone. A sheet of glass or acetate with tiny patterns that act as lenses through which an image is photographed to produce a halftone. Digital screens are now part of computer publishing and printing software.

screen angle Angle at which halftone dots are placed on a page. A 45-degree angle is normally used to produce the illusion of grayscale. In four-color CMYK printing, each color has a different screen angle.

selection area The part of the HP DeskScan preview scan that you select to be saved to a file or sent directly to a printer.

shadow Shadows are the darkest part of a photograph or scanned image.

sharpening A software process that sharpens an image by increasing the contrast of adjacent pixels. Sharpening is an option in both HP DeskScan II software and in image editors such as Photoshop.

SCSI Abbreviation for *Small Computer System Interface*. A computer industry interface standard used for connecting peripherals to personal computers. The HP ScanJet scanner is connected to your personal computer with a SCSI interface.

TIFF Abbreviation for *Tag Image File Format*. A graphic file format originally developed by the Aldus Corporation (now part of Adobe) specifically for scanned images. Now TIFF is a graphic standard image file format that is supported by almost all applications, printers, and scanners.

TWAIN   TWAIN is a software interface standard that lets you scan images from a scanning application such as HP DeskScan II directly into an application like Adobe Photoshop or Corel PHOTO-PAINT.

vector   An image type that consists of lines and curves. A vector graphic can be
graphic   scaled to a larger or smaller size without losing resolution or looking jagged.

Windows   A graphics file format developed by Microsoft for use with Microsoft
bitmap   Windows. Sometimes referred to by its DOS file extension: BMP.

zoom   A DeskScan II software feature used to enlarge the view of the selected part of an image in the Preview area.

INDEX

D

E

F

S

T

U

V

W

Z